The Impresario's Ten Commandments

ROYAL MUSICAL ASSOCIATION MONOGRAPHS

General Editor: David Fallows

This series is supported by funds made available to the Royal Musical Association from the estate of Thurston Dart, former King Edward Professor of Music in the University of London. The editorial board is the Publications Committee of the Association.

No. 1: Playing on Words: a Guide to Luciano Berio's *Sinfonia* (1985) by David Osmond-Smith
No. 2: The Oratorio in Venice (1986) by Denis and Elsie Arnold
No. 3: Music for Treviso Cathedral in the Late Sixteenth Century: a Reconstruction of the Lost Manuscripts 29 and 30 (1987) by Bonnie J. Blackburn
No. 4: The Breath of the Symphonist: Shostakovich's Tenth (1988) by David Fanning
No. 5: The Song of the Soul: Understanding *Poppea* (1992) by Iain Fenlon and Peter N. Miller
No. 6: The Impresario's Ten Commandments: Continental Recruitment for Italian Opera in London 1763-64 (1992) by Curtis Price, Judith Milhous and Robert D. Hume

ROYAL MUSICAL ASSOCIATION
MONOGRAPHS
6

The Impresario's Ten Commandments

Continental Recruitment for Italian Opera in London 1763-64

CURTIS PRICE, JUDITH MILHOUS

and ROBERT D. HUME

Royal Musical Association
London
1992

Published by the Royal Musical Association
Registered office 41 Vine Street, London EC3N 2AA

© The Royal Musical Association 1992

British Library Cataloguing in Publication Data

A catalogue record for this book is available from the British Library

ISBN 0-947854-05-3

Typeset at the Pennsylvania State University Center for Academic Computing with the assistance of Thomas Minsker
Produced by Alan Sutton Publishing, Stroud, Glos.

Copies may be obtained from:
Brian Jordan (agent)   or RMA Secretary (members)
12 Green Street
Cambridge CB2 3JU

Contents

Preface	v
1 Recruitment for the King's Theatre Season of 1763-64	1
Giardini becomes Impresario	2
Leone's Engagements	6
Composers	14
2 Giardini v. Leone	18
The Venture Unravels	18
The Aftermath	21
Conclusion	26
Appendix A: Giardini's Book of Instructions and Correspondence	36
Appendix B: Leone's Contracts with Performers	78
Index	90

For Winton, Thalia and Stephen

Preface

Italian opera was a conspicuous part of musical life in London throughout the eighteenth century. The King's Theatre in the Haymarket, the principal venue for foreign opera, was the capital's most glamorous and prestigious theatre. A satellite of the Court and a magnet for the rich and powerful, it was often able to attract the greatest performers at the highest salaries paid anywhere in Europe, despite the lack of state subsidy. At other times it struggled merely to stay in business, not always with success. The King's Theatre, which was a premier Italian opera house, nevertheless laboured under a serious disadvantage: it had to import virtually all its performers and repertory. London was remote from the mainstream of opera, necessitating the expense and hazards of international travel. Another problem was the King's Theatre's long season (from November to July), which cut across Carnival and the numerous other short festivals during which opera was traditionally performed in Italy. These complications made planning extremely difficult for a London impresario.

The recruitment of composers and singers remains the least investigated aspect of Italian opera in eighteenth-century England. We rarely know the performers' salaries, let alone the contractual details of their conditions of employment in London. The period between the collapse of Lord Middlesex's company in the 1740s and William Taylor's regime in the 1780s and 1790s is particularly perplexing and obscure. The recent publication of Drummonds Bank accounts relating to the King's Theatre, Haymarket, and some of its personnel in the 1760s and 1770s is welcome, but it gives only a tantalizing glimpse of the company's operations.[1] One would like to know, for example, how the theatre recruited singers and dancers, how much it paid them, and what was expected of house composers at a time when the pasticcio reigned supreme in London. The heretofore unknown letters and contracts that form the basis of this monograph constitute a major addition to our still slender store of knowledge about these subjects.

---

[1] See Elizabeth Gibson, 'Italian opera in London, 1750-1775: management and finances', *Early Music*, 18 (1990), 47-59.

The Impresario's Ten Commandments

In June 1763 the well-known violinist Felice Giardini received a licence from the Lord Chamberlain to mount a season of Italian opera and ballet at the King's Theatre. He had some knowledge of the opera house, having served as leader of the pit orchestra between 1754 and 1757, and as co-manager of the company in 1756-57. In the summer of 1763 he found himself fully occupied in London and so sent a friend, Gabriele Leone, to engage appropriate performers in Italy. But the singers and dancers Leone recruited were not of the first rank, and most of them proved unpopular. Not surprisingly, Giardini lost money. Upon discovering in March 1764 that Leone had collected kickbacks from some of the performers, Giardini sued; the performers counter-sued to collect their salaries; and in September Leone replied with a long and detailed pamphlet (apparently extant in only one copy) in which he printed Giardini's instructions and letters to him *in extenso*.

The row dragged on into 1765 (in court and in print), but reached no legal resolution. Giardini's frank and apparently uncensored letters, however, were preserved, and they constitute a marvellously vivid and detailed source of information about the world of eighteenth-century Italian opera, both in Italy and in London. The letters reveal much about the unscrupulous practices of singers and impresarios in making engagements; how singers were selected and operas commissioned; what composers thought about the London pasticcio system. They provide new information about Johann Christian Bach, Niccolò Piccinni and Mattia Vento; they also give us financial and personal details about numerous singers and dancers—both those hired by Giardini and those unsuccessfully recruited.

Taken in chronological order, the principal documents are as follows.

(1) A Chancery lawsuit, Giardini v. Leone, Vento, Guglietti, Marcucci, Mazziotti and Baini (London, Public Record Office C 12/521/4). Bill of complaint filed 26 March 1764; various answers filed 28 May 1764 to 12 February 1765. Leone's answer is filed separately as C 12/517/16 (3 August 1764).

(2) Giardini's angry notice in the *Public Advertiser* of 9 May 1764.

(3) A reply by Leone, et al., in the *Public Advertiser* of 14 May 1764.

(4) The *Réponse à un avertissement très-insolent . . . par Felice Giardini* (London: [no publisher], 1764), said to be written and compiled by Gabriele Leone but allegedly ghost-written by 'Cacophron'. (See Ill. 1 and Ill. 5.)

(5) A counter-suit: Mazziotti, Baini, Guglietti, Marcucci and Vento v. Giardini (C 12/1008/4). Bill of complaint filed 1 June 1764; answer filed on 4 December 1764.

(6) R. P., *A Defence of F. Giardini, from the Calumnies, Falshoods, and Misrepresentations, of Cacophron* (London: R. Davis, 1765).[2]

Many of the letters included in Leone's answer (C 12/517/16) are also printed in the *Réponse*, but the pamphlets and lawsuits are supplementary and each provides information not found in the other.

The lawsuits yield copies of several contracts—the earliest extant for any group of King's Theatre performers. The first part of this study tells the story of Giardini's management and analyzes the new documents. Appendix A is a bilingual edition of the opera correspondence (with some explanatory annotation); Appendix B contains transcriptions and translations of the performers' contracts. These documents tell us a great deal about a particular and hitherto almost unnoticed season; they also provide the foundations for a study of international recruiting. We hope that as other such documents come to light the present study may help form the basis for a broader reassessment of artistic policy and foreign recruitment for the Italian opera in London in the eighteenth century.

Acknowledgments

For invaluable assistance in dealing with the faulty Italian texts in Appendices A and B we are much indebted to the generosity of Lowell Lindgren, John Rosselli and Antonietta Cerocchi Pozzi. Pierre Danchin graciously helped us with the translation of the French in 'Graziani's statement'. For expert advice on the identification of singers and dancers we wish to thank John Rosselli, Pierluigi Petrobelli and Antonietta Cerocchi Pozzi. Rhian Samuel and Kit Hume offered cogent critiques of early drafts of our narrative. Tom Minsker gave us invaluable assistance with the printing.

We are indebted to the Controller of Her Majesty's Stationery Office for permission to print Crown Copyright documents from the Public Record Office.

The research and writing for this monograph were carried out under a generous grant from the National Endowment for the Humanities.

---

[2] Both pamphlets are briefly mentioned in Simon McVeigh, *The Violinist in London's Concert Life 1750-1784* (New York: Garland, 1989), p. 159, n. 48. James Fullarton Arnott and John William Robinson, *English Theatrical Literature 1559-1900: A Bibliography* (London: Society for Theatre Research, 1970), list only the *Defence of F. Giardini* (no. 1454).

Works Frequently Cited

Biographical Dictionary——Philip H. Highfill, Jr., Kalman A. Burnim and Edward A. Langhans, *A Biographical Dictionary of Actors, Actresses, Singers, Dancers, Managers, and other Stage Personnel in London, 1660-1800*, 16 vols. in progress (Carbondale, Il.: Southern Illinois University Press, 1973-)

DEUMM——*Dizionario Enciclopedico Universale della Musica e dei Musicisti*, 12 vols. and supplement, ed. Alberto Basso (Torino: UTET, 1983-1990)

Horace Walpole's Correspondence——*The Yale Edition of Horace Walpole's Correspondence*, ed. W. S. Lewis, et al., Vol. XXXVIII (London: Oxford University Press, 1974)

The London Stage——*The London Stage, 1660-1800*, Part 4: 1747-1776, 3 vols., ed. George Winchester Stone, Jr. (Carbondale: Southern Illinois University Press, 1962)

New Grove——*The New Grove Dictionary of Music and Musicians*, 20 vols., ed. Stanley Sadie (London: Macmillan, 1980)

Réponse——*Réponse à un avertissement très-insolent . . . par Felice Giardini* (London, 1764)

Sartori——Claudio Sartori, *I libretti italiani a stampa dalle origini al 1800* (Cuneo: Bertola e Locatelli, 1991-)

Wiel——Taddeo Wiel, *I teatri musicali Veneziani del settecento* (Venice, 1897, rpt Bologna: A. Forni, 1978)

1
Recruitment for the King's Theatre Season of 1763-64

In the 1750s the King's Theatre was in the doldrums. Following the collapse of the Middlesex regime in the mid-1740s management seemed to have become permanently unstable, and the company often had to be run by the artists themselves. The audience wanted star singers and dancers, and the opera company recruited them as best it could. Nonetheless, principal performers rarely stayed more than a season or two, despite salaries that were sometimes extremely generous. By comparison, composers were a very low priority, little esteemed and poorly paid: the dominance of the pasticcio had reduced them to mere arrangers of extant music and suppliers of linking *secco* recitative. The whole venture was manifestly shaky. Each season the undertaker had to raise sufficient capital to engage performers who could attract enough subscribers to convince the Lord Chamberlain that the venture could pay its bills and should receive a licence.

Managers came and went. On and off between 1750 and 1759 the principal undertaker was Francesco Vanneschi, a former librettist who had succeeded the ill-fated Giovanni Francesco Crosa.[1] In 1754 Vanneschi appointed Giardini leader of the King's Theatre orchestra. According to Burney, the spirited and temperamental violinist 'introduced new discipline, and a new style of playing, much superior in itself, and more congenial with the poetry and music of Italy, than the languid manner of his predecessor Festing'.[2] Vanneschi also hired the

---
[1] For an account of Crosa's tenure as manager, see Saskia Willaert, 'The first Italian comic operas in London, 1748-1750', Master's dissertation, King's College London (1990).
[2] Charles Burney, *A General History of Music* (1789; rpt. New York: Dover, 1957), II, 853.

celebrated contralto Regina Mingotti as *prima donna* for the same season (1754-55), but the two soon fell out; after a very public quarrel, Vanneschi went bankrupt and followed Dr Crosa into ignominious exile on the Continent.[3] Giardini and Mingotti became co-managers in 1756-57 but resigned when receipts did not match the 'great applause' which Burney accorded their productions. Mingotti and Giardini were in turn succeeded by another performer-manager team, the soprano Colomba Mattei and her husband Joseph Trombetta, though Peter Crawford served as partner and treasurer and Vanneschi returned briefly as licensee.[4] Their regime was distinguished by unusual attention to repertory and an attempt to return some status to the composer in a theatre which had long relied mainly on pasticcios. They engaged Gioacchino Cocchi as music director in 1757, reintroduced comic opera in 1760-61, and brought J. C. Bach to London for the first time during the 1762-63 season. This period of relative stability and artistic distinction came to an end because the proprietors were losing money. In a notice in the *Public Advertiser* of 13 July 1763 Crawford and Trombetta announced that the 'Partnership' between them 'is now dissolved' and informed the public that though 'so very large a Sum as almost Two Thousand Pounds appears against us . . . as our Books shew, which are ready for Inspection . . . We yet have been able to pay all our just Debts', and they invited any remaining claimants to apply for their money. The decision to bail out had been made some time earlier. On 31 May the opera advertisement in the *Public Advertiser* had concluded with a special notice:

N.B. *As Signora Mattei will leave England soon after the Operas are over; and as Mr. Crawford intends to have no farther Concern with the Management of Operas, all the Cloaths used in the Burlettas and Dances, with many other Articles, being his Property and that of Signora Mattei's, WILL BE SOLD.*

The field was open for a new impresario, and we may deduce that the eager Giardini had already decided to concentrate on *opera seria*, no doubt arranging to take over that part of the company's stock of costumes and letting his predecessors sell the rest. Why he did not want their dance costumes we do not know.

Giardini becomes Impresario

In early July 1763 Giardini found himself in sole control of the King's

---

[3] McVeigh, p. 157.
[4] See *The London Stage*, II, 681, and *Survey of London*, Vol. XXIX (London: Athlone Press, 1960), 229. The licence is in P.R.O. LC 5/162, p. 92 (16 May 1757).

Theatre.[5] Flush with enthusiasm and headstrong with power, he failed fully to appreciate the difficulties he faced. The popular *prima donna* Signora Mattei was preparing to return to the Continent, and so was Bach, whose serious opera *Orione* had been 'extremely applauded by a very numerous audience', while his *Zanaida* had just closed the season on 11 June. However, Giardini shrugged off the departure of La Mattei and Bach: he wanted to sweep away the cobwebs of the old management and was determined to engage a completely new troupe. In a letter of 15 July 1763 he wrote: 'Trombetta, Mattei, and Bach are set out this day for Paris—great regrets and lamentations, but easily dried up without a great handkerchief' ('Grandissimi pianti, ma che si potevano asciugare senza gran fazzoletto').[6] Giardini was capable of composing substitute arias and assembling pasticcios himself, but he wanted a big-name composer to replace Bach—to wit, Piccinni.

Mid-July was rather late to start assembling a company.[7] As early as 3 March 1763 Giardini had been running notices in the *Public Advertiser* requesting the 'Nobility and Gentry . . . to pay in Half their Subscription' for the ensuing season 'to enable him to give Security for the Payment of several of the most eminent Singers from Italy'. He adds that he 'would not have presumed to make this early Application to the Public, had he not already received the Sanction of a Licence from the Lord Chamberlain'. But, for whatever reason (possibly the subscribers were unforthcoming), Giardini made no move to assemble a company in the spring. Since he aspired to better performers than were available in London, he chose to let some principal performers go and kept others dangling. Not until mid-July, however, did he start to arrange to look abroad, and by then foreign recruitment was a matter of urgency.

Giardini had probably toured the Continent in search of performers as recently as summer 1756,[8] so he had contacts in Paris and in most of the Italian opera centres. He was, however, swamped with work in London and so decided to employ an agent. Gabriele Leone had come to England from France in September 1762 under the protection of the Duke of Nivernois.[9] A music teacher and occasional concert performer, Leone soon became a close associate of Giardini, who liked to surround himself with compatriots. The tone of Giardini's early letters shows that the two men were good friends—the

---

[5] *The London Stage*, II, 1007 (following Burney, II, 867), incorrectly states that Mingotti once again joined Giardini in the opera government.
[6] See Appendix A, No. XXI.
[7] In 1788 William Taylor testified that Easter was 'the proper time of making Engagements with performers abroad for the season afterwards' (C31/251, no. 207). We assume this was equally true in the 1760s.
[8] McVeigh, p. 157.
[9] *Réponse*, pp. 4-5.

manager provided money for Leone's family and chided him for neglecting his wife—and the agent at first enjoyed Giardini's complete confidence, bearing a power of attorney to use on his travels.[10] Nevertheless, Giardini prudently drew up a detailed Book of Instructions, complete with itinerary, an extensive list of contacts, preferred performers (both named individuals and the qualities desired), a blank contract, a salary schedule (with a formula for augmentation should haggling be necessary), a letter of introduction and a list of merchants and bankers from whom Leone could supposedly draw earnest money and cash to cover travel expenses. Giardini also provided 'The Ten Commandments' for the novice foreign opera agent (see Appendix A, No. IX):

    I. To discover no secrets.
    II. Never to be hasty.
    III. Not to treat with buffos.
    IV. To be civil to all.
    V. To talk little, and hearken a great deal.
    VI. Œconomy with Decorum.
    VII. To remember what is said.
    VIII. To open your Ears more than your Eyes.
    IX. Who serves a true Friend, obliges himself.
    X. When Things go well, you will have Honour and Profit.

As we shall see, these commandments in no way prepared Leone for the cut-throat business which lay ahead, and Giardini was soon urging his agent to break most of them.

Leone was instructed to assemble a full company of principals for *opera seria* (comic opera was not yet firmly established in London); a composer (Piccinni, if available); *primo uomo*; *prima donna*; *seconda donna*; *terza donna*; bass; tenor; two promising young female singers; and two comic dancers. He left London on 12 July 1763, a month after the season had closed, and his problems began almost immediately. At Paris Madame Grasse refused to honour Giardini's letter of credit for 300 French *livres* (£13 2s 6d)—according to a pro-Giardini pamphlet, because she 'knew Leone, who had resided some Years at Paris, much better than Giardini knew him'.[11] Anxious to avoid delay and having already spent the 15 guineas he had been advanced in London, Leone claimed to have paid his own way to Turin by selling his personal effects, 'even my Cloaths'.[12] He was still able to travel in some comfort—by post-chaise to Lyons and by hired carriages 'to

---

[10] *Réponse*, pp. 24-25; a copy is in C 12/1008/4 (answer). See Appendix A, No. Ia.
[11] *A Defence of F. Giardini*, p. 4.
[12] *Réponse*, p. 9; Leone's answer to Giardini's bill of complaint (C 12/517/16) given under oath, tells a slightly different story: 'he [Leone] was obliged to take up goods on his own credit at Paris and sell many of them for less than prime cost.'

pass the mountain'.[13] The main cities in which he was to recruit performers were Bologna, Rome and Naples but, according to his instructions, Leone was to go first to Milan to hear a young tenor called Cataneo, a pupil of Ferdinando Brivio (presumably Giuseppe Ferdinando Brivio),[14] and other singers (see Appendix A, No. VI). Giardini asked Leone to acquire copies of the scores of recent serious operas and to locate a *Dies illa* by Palladini and any other pieces with grand choruses.[15] The agent was also supposed to greet 'Signor Martini'; given the obsequiousness and formality of the salutation, this was probably the famous Padre Martini (see Appendix A, No. I).

Almost as soon as Leone departed, Giardini compromised his agent by starting to hire performers on his own, both locally and by correspondence. Even before Leone had reached Paris, Giardini had received negative intelligence from Italy on singers whom he had instructed Leone to hire. Without consulting his agent, Giardini hastily signed contracts in London with Giuseppe Giustinelli as second man, Angiola Sartori as second woman and Clementina Cremonini as third woman, boasting in a letter of 15 July 1763: 'You see, Leone, I know how to do my own business' (Appendix A, No. XXI). Leone found himself wandering about Italy, dogged by unreliable credit and ever-changing instructions which arrived long after Giardini had already decided to do something else. The performers they acquired between them proved less than satisfactory, and Giardini quite unfairly blamed Leone for the opera's unsuccessful season. Leone was hardly a paragon: he tried to renege on contracts (admittedly following instructions); he extorted kickbacks from the performers he did sign, swearing them to secrecy; and he tarried long in Italy, revelling in the company of beautiful singers and dancers, one of whom, Signora Maria Marcucci, accompanied him on the return journey to London on what Giardini charged were 'very Corrupt Motives'.[16] Reading both sides of the lawsuit testimony, one may deduce that Leone was dishonest (or at least decided to get his own back by crooked means). But Giardini's instructions and letters show that he was too disorganized and impulsive to administer an opera house: within three days of his agent's departure Giardini was signing up singers he had sworn not to employ, and whose replacements Leone

---

[13] C12/517/16.
[14] Prominent Milanese composer and singing teacher. The soprano Radegonda Visconti, who had sung in London and Venice, was his pupil. Brivio may have been in London in 1742-1745. *New Grove*, III, 308-309, gives his date of death as ?c1758, but Giardini's instructions make clear that he was alive in 1763 (Appendix A, No. I).
[15] See Appendix A, No. I. Giardini seems to have been willing to acquire operas piece-meal, which is not surprising since at this time most London operas were pasticcios: singers might provide their own arias from a suitcase, but choruses had to be composed or borrowed. That he would apparently adapt a sacred piece for the stage is, however, remarkable.
[16] C12/1008/4 (answer).

had been commissioned to find. Our concern here, however, is not with the rights and wrongs of the dispute, but with what the surviving documents can tell us about the recruitment of performers at this time.

Leone's Engagements

The success of any eighteenth-century Italian opera company depended heavily upon the *primo uomo*, and Giardini's instructions were in this instance quite specific. He identified four possible castratos in descending order of preference: Luciani, Cattilini, Guarducci[17] and Mazziotti. Leone was authorized to offer Luciani 1800 zecchini or £855 (1 zecchino = 9s 6d), to be increased to 2000 zecchini if necessary. But when Leone met Luciani at Naples (in September?), the singer demanded £1500 and treated Leone's best offer 'with contempt'.[18] Guarducci, whom Leone interviewed at Siena in late August, asked for £1000 though he was already engaged at various opera houses throughout the 1763-64 season; his apparent willingness to break existing contracts in order to accept a better offer was, as we shall see, common practice at the time. Cattilini was in Spain and unavailable for the next season. There remained the young Antonio Mazziotti, a member of the royal chapel at Naples (not, apparently, the singer of the same name who had sung at the Teatro delle Dame at Rome in 1743). Besides his original instructions (see Appendix A, No. V), Leone was further encouraged to approach this singer by Giardini's letter of 21 July 1763. The manager had received advice from several London businessmen: 'The Day before Yesterday I was informed by many in the City, that this Mazziotti and Guarducci are really the best Singers' (Appendix A, No. XXII). At Naples on 22 September Leone duly engaged Mazziotti as first man 'in heroic operas' for 1500 zecchini; his contract guaranteed a benefit performance and travel expenses, though the agent was forbidden to offer either perquisite.[19] Mazziotti's contract also required him to sing in day-time concerts at the opera house and anywhere else the manager desired.[20]

What happened after the contract was signed and sealed is the subject of dispute. Leone maintained that, acting in Giardini's interests, he persuaded Mazziotti to accept a 300 zecchini abatement of his salary by warning him that unless artists' expenses were reduced the

---

[17] Presumably Tommaso Guarducci, who came to London in 1766-67 (see *The London Stage*, II, 1182).
[18] C 12/517/16.
[19] Giardini expressly forbade Leone to promise any performer clothing, lodging or travel expenses, but simply 'qualche piccola cosa di più' (Appendix A, No. VII).
[20] Copies of the contract are in C 12/521/4 (Mazziotti's answer) and in C 12/517/16; see Appendix B, No. I.

whole enterprise might fail.[21] The mechanism by which this alleged 'abatement' occurred was that Mazziotti signed a receipt for a 300 zecchini salary advance that he did not receive. Other performers made similar deals.[22] Giardini later charged Leone with extorting kickbacks. An advertisement in the *Public Advertiser* of 9 May 1764 (reprinted in the *Réponse*, pp. 2-3) asks:

Whether some of [the performers engaged by Leone] *did*, or *did not* give Mr. *Giardini*'s agent a *receipt for money*, which they had not *received*, nor ever were to *receive*; with a view that the agent might charge Mr. *Giardini* with these sums.

Giardini insisted in lawsuit testimony that neither Leone nor the performers had informed him of the 'reduced' contracts, and that Leone had charged him the full total of the receipts on the advances he had given. The performers in question denied Giardini's accusation, and Leone side-stepped the charge in both the lawsuits and in his *Réponse à un avertissement très-insolent*. Leone's story, however, seems virtually impossible to credit: we can see no plausible reason other than fraud for his extorting receipts for money he had not paid. Whether, as Giardini charges, he hired bad performers because they were willing to agree to pay him kickbacks is impossible to determine.

Mazziotti was apparently not much of a success in London, though evidence of critical reception during the 1763-64 season is extremely scarce. Burney does not comment on the quality of the singers but calls the season 'inauspicious'.[23] Horace Walpole, who was ill-disposed towards Giardini ('I would not go cross the room to hear him play to eternity') and offended by his attempts to stampede the gentry into subscribing to the opera,[24] pronounced the season a failure after only two nights. In a letter to the Earl of Hertford of 2 December 1763, he wrote: 'The first man [Mazziotti], though with sweet notes, has so weak a voice that he might as well hold his tongue.' In his original lawsuit[25] Giardini did not comment on the castrato's ability, but in a later reply to a counter-suit brought by several of the performers,[26] he lashed out at Mazziotti: how could such a poor singer ever have been in the service of the King of Naples? He 'never Sung on any Stage as Principal Singer before he came to

---

[21] *Réponse*, pp. 14-17.
[22] *Réponse*, pp. 18-19.
[23] *A General History*, II, 867. *The London Stage*, II, 1035, prints a report under 21 January 1764 of 'The great concourse of people at this theatre before the usual time of opening the doors'. The editor fails to explain, however, that the crowd came to see the Prince of Brunswick (who had just married George III's sister).
[24] *Horace Walpole's Correspondence*, XXXVIII, 208-09, letter of 9 August 1763 to the Hon. Henry Seymour Conway.
[25] C12/521/4, 26 March 1764.
[26] C12/1008/4, 4 December 1764.

England Save that he Sung one Season in that Capacity in the City of Genoa where he was not liked'. Mazziotti had earlier provided a *curriculum vitae*[27] (the Genoa season is not mentioned) which claims that the nobility of Gubbio had paid him 120 zecchini for only three days' work in May 1761, that his usual fee was 15-20 zecchini per night and that he was particularly well received by the Prince of Francavilla and the Duke of Maddaloni—credentials hardly likely to impress an audience who could hear Tenducci almost any night at Covent Garden and some of whom still remembered Farinelli. In the legal wrangling Mazziotti was even attacked by his colleague Mingotti, who described him as 'but a Middling Singer' who would be lucky to earn 300 zecchini per year at Rome or Naples.[28]

There was less urgency over the negotiations to secure a *prima donna*, a charge which was in Leone's brief until the end of August 1763. Agent and manager had agreed first to approach Signora Spagnioletta (called La Brucciatina), and Leone accordingly wrote to her in Venice from Bologna in early August.[29] Explaining his failure to engage her, Leone claimed that Giardini had refused to advance him any earnest money.[30] At the time, neither man seemed particularly worried; the reason for their complacency becomes clear in Giardini's letter of 30 August 1763: 'If you have not fixed with the Spagnioletta, (as it seems) do not engage any one as I shall have the Mingotti. Here we are then safe in port' (Appendix A, No. XXVIII). Giardini's former partner in management was a reliable and probably economical option, though now past her prime. Walpole complained: 'The Mingotti, whom [Giardini] has forced upon the town, is as much disliked as if he had insisted on her being first lord of the Treasury.'[31]

Before receiving Giardini's letter of 30 August 1763 which instructed him not to engage *any* woman singer, Leone had travelled on to Rome. There he signed Cecilia Baini for 500 zecchini, though he says he could have offered her as much as 1000,[32] the amount Giardini had authorized for a 'middling' singer (Appendix A, No. VII). Despite the manager's instruction not to specify any singer's rank 'with respect to the rest', except for *primo uomo* and *prima donna*, Baini's contract imprudently includes a clause granting her an extra 100 zecchini 'in case she shall be Employed as first woman Singer'.[33]

---

[27] C12/521/4 (answer of 28 May 1764).
[28] Deposition sworn on 30 June 1764 on behalf of Giardini: C24/1739.
[29] C12/517/16.
[30] Ibid. 'Signora Brucciatina' is evidently the Clementina Spagnioli who wrote to Leone on 27 August 1763 declining his invitation because of prior engagements (not lack of earnest money). See Appendix A, No. XXVIIb.
[31] *Horace Walpole's Correspondence*, XXXVIII, 250.
[32] C12/517/16.
[33] See Appendix B, No. II.

Leone then forced Baini and her husband (who acted as her agent) to accept a 50 zecchini abatement in salary—or to pay him a kickback, depending on whose story one prefers to believe. Mingotti described her colleague as 'very indifferent',[34] and Giardini claimed that she was 'a very bad' singer[35] who had 'never Attempted to Sing in Public before the said pretended Agreement [was signed] and is absolutely unqualified for it'.[36] This was an exaggeration, since Baini performed regularly throughout the 1763-64 season in London, though with no apparent distinction.

Leone's negotiations over a bass singer reveal another aspect of the ugly ethics of Italian opera at this time and also tell us how this voice type was regarded. After auditioning at least two basses in Naples, including Carmine Bagniani and Nicola Pellegrini, the agent engaged the latter for 400 zecchini on 23 September 1763.[37] Soon afterwards, however, he 'heard [Domenico] *Guglietti*, and preferring his Voice, endeavoured to be off with *Pellegrini*; but he had already received Earnest, and had recourse to the Law to oblige me to maintain the Contract'. Counting legal costs and compensation, Leone had to pay out at least £30 17s 6d to get rid of Pellegrini.[38] Leone admits that Guglietti was no great singer, but says that Giardini never intended a bass should supply the place of a tenor; rather, the bass was to sing mainly in choruses. Guglietti himself adds credence to the surprising story that Giardini was prepared to pay as much as 400 zecchini for a mere chorister. Arriving in London on 9 November 1763, he auditioned for Giardini and was indeed consigned to the chorus when the season began on 26 November. However, as the season progressed, Guglietti says that he was called upon 'sometimes to Act Parts in the Operas', which presumably meant solo roles.[39] His only known role was in Vento's *Leucippo*: Narete, a major part and surprisingly demanding for one so inexperienced. He claims also to have taken part in *Siroe*, *Senocrita*, 'and afterwards in *Alexander*' (that is, in a revival of Cocchi's *Alessandro nell'Indie*).[40]

This was not Giardini's original plan: he had set aside 550 zecchini for a tenor and had written to one Romani, 'the famous Tenor in the King of Prussia's service', before Leone left London. The

---

[34] C24/1739.
[35] C12/521/4 (bill of complaint).
[36] C12/1008/4 (answer).
[37] C12/517/16; *Réponse*, pp. 14-15; and especially C12/521/4.
[38] That is, 75 ducats earnest money; 130 ducats compensation; and 75 zecchini legal expenses. *Réponse*, pp. 14-15; C12/517/16.
[39] C12/521/4 (answer of Guglietti and Marcucci). For his contract, see Appendix B, No. III.
[40] Guglietti's year in London has not previously been noticed. Giardini did not usually advertise casts, and the editor of *The London Stage* failed to look at the printed librettos. Consequently the authors of the *Biographical Dictionary* were not aware of his presence.

following excerpts from Giardini's letters tell a story of disappointment: 'I am in constant expectation of *Romani*'s final answer; if he does not return me the contract, as soon as ever the time is expired, I will tell you what to do' (15 July 1763, No. XXI); '*Romani* . . . is this Day *confirmed* to me, and *I have his Contract*, so that we *need think no more about a Tenor*' (21 July 1763, No. XXII); '*Romani comes*' (22 August 1763, No. XXVI); 'Romani comes, so that I want only a first man, a first Woman . . . and a Bass' (late August? 1763, No. XXVII); 'I Am just assured the King of Prussia intends to have an Opera, and that *I cannot have Romani*. Therefore endeavour to have a *Tenor*, and take *Cattaneo* if you cannot get a better' (23 September 1763, No. XXXII, written for Giardini by his assistant manager, Pietro Giovanetti). On his way back to London, Leone made a half-hearted attempt to engage the only unemployed tenor he could find, Gaetano Ottani, but he demanded £1000 and Leone lacked the earnest money.[41] Ottani sang at the Teatro Regio, Turin, throughout the 1750s and 1760s. In certain continental opera houses tenors, notably the great Anton Raaff, were beginning to vie with the castratos for top billing.[42] However, nearly 30 years would pass before a tenor (Giacomo Davide) would supplant the *primo uomo* at the King's Theatre. Giardini's salary differential—1500 zecchini for Mazziotti as against 550 for Romani—confirms the relatively low esteem in which he held the voice type, even though he expresses admiration for this 'Tenore famosissimo' and regret at not being able to engage him.

Leone's original instructions called for a 'Third Woman' but did not specify an *ultima parte* as such (*Réponse*, pp. 6-7). As early as 15 July, however, Giardini engaged Clementina Cremonini to fill this slot. When her father refused to allow her to join the King's Theatre troupe, Giardini wrote to Leone on 16 September 1763 with a frantic request for him to hire either 'a Woman of a good figure' who could 'occasionally perform in Mens Cloaths' or 'a young Castrato with a good voice' as the *ultima parte* to sing both male and female roles (Appendix A, No. XXXI). Cecilia Baini was eventually bullied into serving in this lowly, dual capacity.[43] She was rather expensive for this position, but that was hardly Leone's fault.

Leone was also instructed to hire two comic dancers for a maximum of 1300 zecchini for both. These negotiations proved especially difficult, because the best dancers came in virtually inseparable pairs; either partner could therefore hold the other to ransom. Once in Italy, Leone wrote to 'a most famous dancer' Gennaro Magri (called Genariello) at Vienna. A copy of Magri's cordial response of 18 August

---

[41] C12/517/16, where the scribe misread the name as 'Offani'.
[42] See Pierluigi Petrobelli, 'The Italian Years of Anton Raaff', *Mozart-Jahrbuch* (1973/74), 233-273.
[43] C12/517/16.

1763 is preserved in Leone's answer to Giardini's bill of complaint:[44] 'with pleasure I would dear ffriend accept your proposal willingly But I am Engaged for the whole year and am well paid and can be here as many Years as I please. . . . I have here six hundred sequins and my Journeys paid.' Nevertheless, Magri was willing to 'apply for Leave' from Vienna and move to London for 700 zecchini and a benefit. In a postscript he noted an obstacle: 'as to the Partner I have at present she will not take such steps at present not knowing who the Managers are or being Acquainted with them and because her Term is not yet finished.' Magri suggested that Leone try to engage Maddalena Formigli ('La Mora') at Venice as a substitute partner, but the agent chose to interpret the dancer's letter as a refusal of his offer. Yet even before he had received Magri's equivocal reply, Leone had attempted to engage Pierre Bernard Michel at Bologna 'about the beginning of August',[45] on Giardini's advice.[46] Leone offered Michel 1200 zecchini. His current partner was Signora Maria Marcucci, then unknown to Leone. Michel signed a contract with her on 14 August 1763 (see Appendix A, No. XXXVI) to perform in London, but when Leone could not produce the 200 zecchini which Michel required as earnest money, the dancer broke off negotiations and Signora Marcucci departed Bologna for Venice, where she was engaged as 'first Grotesque Dancer' at San Moisè.[47] Much later, on 26 October 1763, Leone engaged Signora Marcucci as 'first Comic Woman Dancer' for 450 zecchini, together with her new partner Luigi Berardi for another 200 zecchini.[48] But Leone, apparently failing to appreciate the solidarity amongst dancing partners, had already hired Vincenzo De Bustis (called Ravaschiello) at Naples. All three dancers accompanied Leone as far as Paris, where poor Ravaschiello was abandoned to starve, ostensibly for lack of travel money. Berardi straggled to London at the end of January 1764, where Giardini 'extorted from him a fresh Contract, with a Deduction of about forty five Pounds'.[49] The pamphleteer justifies this on the ground that Berardi had 'loitered at

---

[44] C12/517/16. See Appendix A, No. XXVa, which is Magri's only known letter. He was active in Venice in the early 1760s (see Wiel, pp. 226-227, 229). He was to serve as choreographer and first dancer at the Teatro San Carlo, Naples, in 1766-67 and as choreographer and second dancer there during 1773-74. He later published the important *Trattato teorico-prattico di ballo* (Naples, 1779).
[45] C12/517/16. Michel had worked regularly in Venice from 1760 to 1762. See Wiel, pp. 226-229, 238.
[46] Appendix A, No. XXIII, dated 26 July 1763. Giardini may have heard about Michel from Cosimo Maranesi, 'no great Dancer', who wanted a job in London; the manager decided to keep him 'at Bay' and use him 'as a Foot-ball'.
[47] C12/521/4 (answer of Guglietti and Marcucci). In the context of eighteenth-century dance, 'grotesque' means 'comic'.
[48] For Marcucci's contract, see Appendix B, No. IV. On Berardi, see *Réponse*, pp. 18-19.
[49] *A Defence*, p. 6.

Paris, till the Opera Season was almost half over'. By contrast, Signora Marcucci had travelled in some style with Leone, though in London she fared little better than her colleagues. Despite a respectable minor career which had taken her to Barcelona, Montpellier and Venice under the impresario Grimaldi,[50] she was ill-received. Giardini reported that at the King's Theatre she 'was hissed by the Spectators. And after her Second Attempt to Dance several of the Subscribers did insist upon her Dancing no more'.[51] At this point the ballet master, Pietro Sodi, demoted Signora Marcucci to figurante, an insult which prompted her resignation. She finished the season at Sadler's Wells, which Giardini implies was a theatre of last resort.

Despite Leone's original *carte blanche* for recruiting, he engaged only seven performers, one of whom, Ravaschiello, never reached London. With information from *The London Stage*, the correspondence and lawsuits, the company may be reconstructed. In the list that follows, some of the ranks are speculative (indicated by [brackets]). People not in the *London Stage* roster are indicated with a dagger (†). Those performers hired by Leone are marked with an asterisk (*). We have added full-value salaries (converted to pounds sterling) when known.[52]

The Opera

Antonio Mazziotti*	*primo uomo*	[£712 10s]
Regina Mingotti	*prima donna*	
Angiola Sartori	*seconda donna*	
Giuseppe Giustinelli	*secondo uomo*	
Maddalena Tagnoni	[*terza donna*]	
Niccolò Peretti	?	
Cecilia Baini*	*ultima parte*	[£237 10s]
Domenico Guglietti*	*basso*	[£190]
Mattia Vento*	composer	[£104 10s][53]

---

[50] C12/521/4 (answer of Guglietti and Marcucci).
[51] C12/1008/4 (answer).
[52] Three errors in the roster in *The London Stage* should be noted. Mazziotti is listed as 'Manziotti'; this has created a ghost in the *Index*, p. 543. Among dancers both 'Bernardi' and 'Berardi' are given: the former is a ghost. Also among dancers both 'Pietro' and 'Sodi' are entered, but these are merely first and last names of the same person.
[53] Calculated from 220 zecchini in the second contract. The original (300 zecchini) contract was worth £142 10s.

The Ballet

Pietro Sodi	ballet master
Giovanni Battista Noferi [54]	[leader of the dances?]

Principal dancers
Dauberval	
Maria Marcucci*	[£213 15s]
[replaced by] Miss Janneton Auretti	
Luigi Berardi*	[£95]
James Fishar	

Coryphées
Duvall
Miss LaLauze
Miss Tetley

Orchestra

Felice Giardini	leader of the band
Carlo Graziani	principal cellist

Non-performers

Felice Giardini	Manager
Pietro Giovanetti	Assistant Manager
James Spilsbury†[55]	Treasurer
Joseph Capitani†[56]	Tailor

Leone was also asked to 'enquire after, and treat with some *good Scene-Painter*', though there is no indication that he engaged such a person (see Appendix A, No. XXXII). This late and casual request gives some indication of the relative insignificance of scenery in the London opera of the 1760s.

---

[54] A guitarist, violinist and répétiteur mentioned in various Giardini letters (see, e.g., Appendix A, Nos. XX and XXI).
[55] Spilsbury received a benefit as treasurer on 5 April 1764. We derive his Christian name from a payment in Giardini's Drummonds account.
[56] See Appendix A, Nos. XIX and XXXVII. 'Le Tailleur de l'Opéra' preceded Leone to Paris in June 1763; this was almost certainly Signor Capitani. A distress benefit on 9 June 1763 was advertised in the *Public Advertiser* of 7 June for 'Sig. Capitani Taylor to the Opera for these 20 Years past, now a Prisoner in the King's Bench'. He is omitted from the *Biographical Dictionary*, where he is mentioned only in Polly Capitani's entry (III, 44), because *The London Stage* misreports the benefit advertisement and erroneously terms him 'singer in the Opera' (II, 1000). From a payment listed under Giardini's account at Drummonds, we learn that Capitani's Christian name was Joseph.

Composers

Perhaps the most important information to come out of the Giardini-Leone dispute concerns the status of opera composers at the King's Theatre. We have already seen that J. C. Bach's departure drew only crocodile tears from the new manager. Before Leone set off on his journey, Giardini had apparently been in correspondence with the great Piccinni, by far the most successful Italian opera composer of his generation, or had at least been in touch with someone at Rome with knowledge of his engagements. According to Leone's third instruction, he was to go to Rome to see 'If *Piccini* comes in the Spring'; in other words, Giardini already knew that the composer would be unavailable for the beginning of the season in November 1763. Leone was authorized to offer him £200 for composing two operas and adapting separate arias ('occorrendo qualche arie distaccate'):[57] Piccinni, like Handel and J. C. Bach before him, would be expected to contribute to pasticcios. This interpretation is confirmed by Instruction XII, which is a contingency plan: 'In case *Piccini* should not accept or could not come, to take this *Mattia Vento*, not exceeding the price of 220 Sequins; with an article in his Contract, that he shall be obliged to put Pasticcio's together [and] to compose airs, duets, recitative', as Giardini directs. Note that there is no indication that Vento would be commissioned to compose new operas.[58]

In the *Réponse* Leone says that upon his arrival in Rome (in late August or September 1763), he was 'informed for certain, that *Piccini* could not come', and so immediately engaged Vento, who agreed to break his contract with a Venetian opera house for the next season.[59] Leone was following Giardini's (for once) unequivocal order issued in a letter of 22 August 1763 (Appendix A, No. XXVI):

Do not fail engaging this *Pasticiere* [that is, Vento], and if *Piccini* cannot break off his engagement, endeavour to get his Music. If he will compose an Opera on purpose for me, I will leave him the choice of the Subject, and give him 80 *Sequins* for it. This may gain him credit and acquaintance in this Country, which may prove very beneficial to him against he comes over himself.

Allowing a composer to choose his own libretto was evidently regarded as a considerable inducement; later in the century this was the absolute prerogative of the King's Theatre manager.[60] In another letter (Appendix A, No. XXVII)—undated, but probably written shortly before 22 August 1763—Giardini says: 'With regard to

---

[57] Appendix A, No. III.
[58] On Mattia Vento (1735-1776), see *New Grove*, XIX, 622-623.
[59] *Réponse*, pp. 12-13; see also C12/521/4 (Vento's answer).
[60] For discussion, see Curtis Price, 'Italian Opera and Arson in Late Eighteenth-Century London', *Journal of the American Musicological Society*, 42 (1989), 85-90.

Piccini, certainly I should like to have him; but if that cannot be, it will be necessary to get some of the best entire Operas, and in that case to take [Vento].'[61] In his long answer to Giardini's bill of complaint,[62] Leone states that he went to Venice 'to treat with Piccini the composer to write an opera for Giardini'. But Giardini charged that his agent made no great effort to contact Piccinni, who was 'in the City of Venice at the time . . . Leone was there and the said Leone never spoke to him'.[63]

Vento rejected the terms Leone initially offered him and was apparently offended by being called a *'pasticiere'*. As a 'professor of music', he declined to be engaged 'to compose recitative and put operas together' ('il detto Mattia Vento declinava come professore di musica d'impiegarsi per comporre recitativi e di mettere opere insieme').[64] This could be taken to mean that Vento regarded writing recitative as a menial task best left to assistants; given the context, a more plausible interpretation is that he objected to arranging pasticcios—that is, stringing other composers' arias together with *secco* recitatives, hardly a challenging or a very creative activity. In a letter of 30 August 1763, Giardini softened his position somewhat: 'If you cannot get Piccini, *contract immediately with Mr. Vento*, to compose one Opera, as well as to patch up others [accomodar le altre], and make Recitative, and such other Additions as may be requisite in the course of the Season, and send him away with the rest.' The reason for offering Vento a chance to compose an original work is evident in the next sentence: 'If you can contrive to send them all [that is, Vento and the singers] over by the end of next Month, I might begin my Operas by the end of October, which will be the time of the Princess's Marriage.'[65]

Throughout these exchanges Giardini frequently mentions the pasticcio, the ideal vehicle for placating *virtuosi* determined to sing arias of their own choosing; but he also seems to have recognized the value of mounting a freshly composed opera in celebration of a royal wedding. Vento's *Leucippo* (première 10 January 1764) was a *favola pastorale eroica* set to a libretto by Giovanni Bottarelli. It may not have been composed expressly for the wedding of the Prince of Brunswick and Princess Augusta, King George III's sister, but the newly-weds

---

[61] Of the operas mounted by the King's Theatre in the 1763-64 season, only the pasticcio *Senocrita* (première 21 February) is known to have included music by Piccinni.
[62] C12/517/16.
[63] C12/1008/4 (answer).
[64] C12/517/16.
[65] Appendix A, No. XXVIII. In an earlier, undated letter (No. XXVII) Giardini gives more information: 'It is reported, the King's Sister is to be married in November. If then I could begin my Rehearsals in October, I should find my account in it.' The wedding of Princess Augusta and Ferdinand, hereditary Prince of Brunswick, took place in London in late January 1764.

attended a packed gala performance on 21 January with the rest of the royal family.[66]

Vento's undated first contract testifies to Leone's weakness as an agent.[67] Vento is required to compose two operas 'at the Time it shall be ordered him' by the manager and to assist at all rehearsals; he is to receive 300 zecchini, 100 in advance and 100 for each opera. There is no mention of the other duties which Giardini stipulated in his letters and instructions. Put on the defensive by the later emergence of this contract, Leone was obliged to explain why he had not forced Vento to accept less money, as he had done with others: 'his Salary was so small, that I defy any body to engage a Composer of his FORM to come to London, where every thing is so dear, for so slender an appointment' (*Réponse*, pp. 12-13). Another possible reason for this special treatment might be that Vento was doing Leone's dirty work: for example, the composer was empowered to cancel Cecilia Baini's contract after Leone had left Rome for Naples (*Réponse*, pp. 12-13)—a commission he failed to execute successfully.

Leone claimed that when he arrived in London on 12 December 1763 he could not find a copy of Vento's contract and had forgotten 'the exact terms, or whether he had contracted . . . to compose one or two operas'. When Vento could not produce *his* copy of the contract, Leone, 'imagining that Giardini had in some letter mentioned that he should want but one new opera', quietly drew up a replacement contract with Vento to that effect.[68] This implausible story was corroborated by Vento, who said that 'he this Defendant not recollecting whether by the former Contract he this defendant was to compose one or two operas', he willingly signed a new one.[69] The second contract, which was undated, stipulated that Vento be in London by mid-October 1763 (though he had actually arrived in November); it required him 'to play at all and whatever Rehearsals' and to compose only one opera, all for a salary of 220 zecchini. If Giardini asked him to compose a second opera, then he would receive a further 80 zecchini. Though Vento later found the first contract, thereby exposing Leone's laxity, he vehemently denied any conspiracy to give the agent a cut of his salary. On the contrary, he fulfilled his duties completely in composing *Leucippo* (which did, however, include one aria each by Hasse and Giardini).[70] Vento also played the harpsichord for other operas given during the season 'under the Direction of' Giar-

---

[66] See the *London Chronicle* of 21-24 January 1764 and *Horace Walpole's Correspondence*, XXXVIII, 288-289.
[67] See Appendix B, No. V.
[68] See Appendix B, No. VI.
[69] C12/521/4 (answer of Vento).
[70] See Frederick C. Petty, *Italian Opera in London 1760-1800* ([Ann Arbor:] UMI Research Press, 1980), p. 104.

dini, even though they were the work of other composers.[71] Giardini remarked dismissively that Vento was 'a Young Man very little known' when he arrived in London[72] but he made no criticism of Vento's music; in fact, Vento seems to be the only artist who was paid in full for the season.[73] Whatever hard feelings the lawsuit may have caused between Giardini and Vento were evidently forgotten by 1770 when the two of them jointly advertised a 'Musical Academy' (that is, a concert series) at Mrs Cornelys' concert room in Soho Square.[74]

[71] C12/521/4 (answer of Vento).
[72] C12/521/4 (bill of complaint).
[73] See the answer of Lieutenant-General Sir Robert Rich in C12/521/4 (12 February 1765).
[74] See McVeigh, p. 178. See also Joseph Baretti, *An Account of the Manners and Customs of Italy*, 2nd edn (London: T. Davies, 1769), I, 148.

# 2
# Giardini v. Leone

We turn now to the events of spring 1764. The lawsuits and pamphlets make a sorry catalogue of accusations, recriminations and backbiting—but without them we would have virtually no sources of information about Giardini's management and performers.

The Venture Unravels

As early as the beginning of September 1763 Giardini, buffeted by unwanted advice about singers from Baron Bagge and others, became increasingly snappish in his letters to Leone.[1] He implies with obvious annoyance that his agent was dallying with some young singers and dancers whom he had apparently tried to impress with promises of long-term contracts: 'I entreat you to leave all the Roman Women, though never so handsome, as they are all engaged, and not to think about next year [that is, 1764-65], but about this only. . . . Get to London if possible by the first week in October, or I shall be ruined. . . . If you have any value for me, let us leave off joking.' In a final attempt to pique Leone's conscience, Giardini added, 'Your Wife is well . . . and . . . wants for nothing but your company' (Appendix A, No. XXX).

Both Giardini and Leone took a remarkably cavalier view of contracts. His power of attorney to Leone notwithstanding, Giardini claimed that 'he never gave him [Leone] any Authority to make Contracts in Writing with any performers but only to prevail on them to come to England to Treat with him the said Felice Giardini as to the Conditions of Performance'.[2] This statement is preposterous: no Italian performer would travel to England at the start of the season (even with expenses paid, which Giardini had expressly forbidden) merely to discuss possible conditions of employment. In practice, Giardini

---

[1] See Appendix A, No. XXVI. On Baron Bagge, see Appendix A, note 40.
[2] C12/1008/4 (bill of complaint).

claimed the right to 'ratify' all contracts which had been drawn up in Italy when the performers arrived in London (that is, to cancel or alter them in any way he saw fit). Leone's ethics were no better. For him, a contract was merely a means of hooking a prospective performer in case he could not find a better one—and, of course, an occasion for extorting a kickback. Singers and dancers, as we have seen in the case of Romani and others, were hardly more ethical; they would blithely cancel engagements with the assurance that, in the international world of Italian opera, litigation would be difficult to pursue effectively.

Giardini was ultimately to blame for the failure of the season of 1763-64, and the publication of his letters in autumn 1764 made his impulsiveness, duplicity and incompetence painfully clear.[3] But the correspondence reflects nearly as badly on Leone. He proved naive, indecisive, lazy, unscrupulous and certainly a poor judge of musical talent, except in the case of Vento, who was the only person to emerge from the affair with reputation intact.[4] Leone explains most of his failures as the result of being unable to draw money from various merchants along his route, which criss-crossed Italy from Turin to Naples. There were unquestionably some delays in arranging credit (for which Giardini accepted blame), but as can be seen from the balance sheet reconstructed from lawsuit testimony, Leone did receive substantial sums of money whilst abroad. Leone's own accounts exonerate Giardini of any suspicion of stinginess:[5]

Received from Giardini

	£	s
at London (July 1763)	15	15
at Turin (via Marchesio)	9	10
at Naples and Florence	855	0
at Turin (via post-chaise)	23	12
at Lyons	52	10
at Paris	89	5
at London (for Signora Leone)	10	10
	£1,056	2

---

[3] Leone's statement in the *Réponse* is dated 4 September 1764.
[4] Burney (II, 884): 'Vento's genius never approached the sublime; however, his melody was totally free from vulgarity, and, though not new, was always pleasing and graceful. On which account, and perhaps by the assistance of Italian politics, he had the honour of defeating Bach.'
[5] The following table is a summary of Leone's accounts as recited in his answer to Giardini's suit in C 12/517/16 (3 August 1764); see Ill. 2.

Expended   zecchini

    advances on salary
        Mazziotti   300
        Vento   90
        Baini   100
        Ravaschiello   50
        Guglietti (& Pellegrini)   100
        Marcucci   30
        Berardi   5
        music copied for Giardini   10
                                       ———
                                       685   = £325   7
    travel and accommodation[6]   505   18
    merchandise shipped from Naples[7]   254   3
                                                 ————
                                                £1,085   8

The discrepancy was a mere £29 6s; Giardini sued Leone in order to expose the alleged 'Oath of Secresy' between agent and performers and to recover the kickbacks or 'abatements' of salary that Leone had pocketed.

Leone never admitted receiving any money from those he had engaged, but the accounts suggest otherwise. Did Giardini in fact pay him for his services? A five per cent commission would have been quite normal for an independent agent in Italy around this time.[8] Giardini claims to have agreed to give Leone 'One Guinea for every Day which he should be employed in the said Business . . . as

---

[6] We give only the total: Leone supplies a 23-item list of expenses.

[7] Leone bought various items for Giardini and shipped a large container of merchandise from Naples to London (see Ill. 3). He gives an exhaustive list of these items (some theatrical, some personal) in C12/517/16. Confirmatory testimony concerning these purchases was provided by a fencing master, Gennaro Biasco Celestini, in a deposition made on 30 May 1764 (C24/1736). The goods bought and shipped by Leone included jewelry, trinkets, 'a Stomacher of false stones second hand for the Theatre set in silver' ('una pettina di brilli usata per il Teatro legata in argento'), several oil paintings (including a Virgin by Domenichino [that is, Domenico Zampieri, d. Naples 1641, called 'il Domenichino']—40 zecchini—and 'an Original Picture from 4 to 5 Spans representing a Sampson in the act of Breaking his Chains'—15 zecchini, six 'Fidle Bows of Serpentine Ebony with screws' (worth 12 ducats) and assorted music ('Symphonia & airs' worth 26 ducats). The total value was 319 ducats or £254 3s. In a letter of 30 August 1763 Giardini advised Leone on how he might avoid paying import duty on these goods (see Appendix A, No. XXVIII). Though he printed the incriminating passage in capital letters, there is no sign in the correspondence that Leone was anything but a willing conspirator in these affairs.

[8] See John Rosselli, *The Opera Industry in Italy from Cimarosa to Verdi* (Cambridge: Cambridge University Press, 1984), Chapter 6.

a Satisfaction for his . . . Trouble therein and to defray the Expenses of his Journey'.[9] Leone denied this arrangement ever existed, saying that he would not have undertaken the trip on such terms: as 'Master of Musick he commonly earned six guineas a week from his scholars besides performing occasionally for hire in concerts'.[10] Leone was on the Continent for some 154 days (from 12 July to 12 December 1763), which would have earned him £161 14s, according to Giardini's proffered rate of pay. From the carefully itemized lists appended to Leone's answer to Giardini's lawsuit,[11] his personal expenses can be calculated at about £250 (see Ill. 2). At a guinea per day Leone would have been nearly £100 out of pocket for expenses and would have received nothing at all for his time and trouble.

Despite Leone's persistent denial of wrongdoing and frank accounting of his expenses, there is strong evidence that he did receive kickbacks from the performers he engaged. In depositions sworn on 30 June 1764,[12] Regina Mingotti and Joseph, Count Piossasque, claimed that two performers broke the oath of silence.[13] Mazziotti 'Chattered and Discovered the Affair which he had upon his Word of Honour and by Oath promised to keep secret', namely, that he would give Leone 300 zecchini or some proportion of his full, contracted salary. According to Mingotti, Guglietti was even more forthcoming with details of how the scheme worked: in Naples at the time he was engaged, the *basso* gave Leone a receipt for 100 zecchini in advance money, when in fact he had received only 25. While the agent thus cheated the manager on several engagements, the sums were relatively small. By March 1764, however, Giardini knew he was in financial trouble and evidently wished to recover what money he could while shedding as much as possible of the blame for the fiasco.

The Aftermath

Giardini's management was in serious difficulty by 26 March 1764, when he filed his bill of complaint against Leone, Mazziotti, Guglietti, Marcucci and the Bainis. He had, nonetheless, to try to complete the subscription season, however low company morale must have been. The final offering of the spring was *Enea e Lavinia*, first performed on

---

[9] C12/521/4 (bill of complaint).
[10] C12/517/16.
[11] C12/517/16, Third Schedule.
[12] C24/1739.
[13] According to E. H. Müller von Asow, 'Regina Mingotti. Eine italienische Primadonna aus österreicher Familie', *Musikblätter* (Berlin, 1950), pp. 79-82, 'Graf Piesasque de Non' (a form of the Piedmontese name Piossasco) was Mingotti's lover and the father of her child, known as 'Samuel von Buckingham'.

5 May and advertised as 'A new Opera composed by Giardini. With two entire new sets of Scenes at the Managers Expense' and 'New Dresses'. The cast is not known. By this time the performers had sued Giardini in King's Bench for salary arrears, for on the day of the première Giardini obtained a Chancery injunction blocking the King's Bench action against him.[14] On 9 May he published a long complaint in the *Public Advertiser*, to which Leone, Mazziotti, Guglietti and Vento replied on the 14th in the same newspaper, bidding him defiance and assuring the public of their confidence that Chancery proceedings would vindicate them. The company somehow kept performing until 12 June, though probably to thin houses: several advertisements at the end of the season state that 'The Subscribers Tickets will be admitted double'. On 1 June the performers had filed their own Chancery counter-suit (C 12/1008/4).

Exactly how much money Giardini lost during the season of 1763-64 cannot be determined. The Drummonds Bank figures prove that he had received at least £1155 in subscriptions (a total of 84 subscribers who actually paid only £13 15s on average). The bank ledgers detail only £531 in payments on the 'opera' account and another £922 on Giardini's own account.[15] Total box office receipts are unknown. Some subscriptions may have been paid directly to the treasurer. Total obligations and actual outgo are equally blank. Virtually all that can be said with assurance is that the Drummonds ledgers for 1765, 1766 and 1767 show Giardini overdrawn to the extent of £602 9s 11d. In 1768 the balance was reduced to £325 19s 11d, and by 1770 Giardini had evidently paid off his overdraft. There is no evidence of what proportion of his bills he finally paid.

Despite the fiasco in 1763-64 Giardini had every intention of carrying on as impresario of the King's Theatre, Haymarket, for the next season. The *Defence of F. Giardini* published on his behalf in the spring of 1765 (p. 10) tells us that

Mr. Giardini having suffered a great Loss by the ill Success of the Opera; and being, in consequence of that Loss, unable to pay his Debts immediately, procured a Meeting of his Creditors. At this Meeting they were informed, that Mr. Giardini had engaged an excellent Company of Performers, for the Opera, for the then ensuing Season, by which he hoped to gain as much as he had lost the preceeding Season.

Giardini offered to assign all profits to the creditors, plus his own earnings from concerts and teaching (reserving only what was 'barely necessary for his Support') in return for a two-year suspension of legal action against him. 'A certain Gentleman', having bought the dancer Berardi's claims, spoke against Giardini's proposal, telling the

---

[14] C 33/421, fol. 412.
[15] Gibson, Appendices.

other creditors that the promised castrato Giovanni Manzuoli would not be coming to London.[16] The gentleman, who was seen to arrive at the meeting arm-in-arm with Signora Sartori, convinced the other creditors that Giardini was bluffing, and the accommodation was refused. This left Giardini a prisoner in his own house, unable to stir for fear of arrest for debt, and he was eventually forced to abandon all hope of managing the opera. In the late spring of 1764, while still hoping to carry on, he evidently toyed with a plan to recoup his fortunes by supplementing the King's Theatre's operatic offerings with English plays, for the *London Chronicle* of 26-29 May 1764 contains the following notice:

There is a report, that plays will be performed next winter at the Opera-house in the Hay-market. It seems the Managers of Covent-garden and Drury-lane Theatres having frequently performed Operas, and the latter having particularly engaged the celebrated Spiletta and her family for the ensuing season, the proprietors of the Opera-house think their province invaded by the Play-houses, and are determined to act Plays four times a week, and Italian Operas twice; to which they affirm they have a right, by virtue of their patent.

Nothing came of this plan: the opera house did not, in fact, possess a patent, and Covent Garden and Drury Lane would have objected strenuously to additional competition in legitimate drama. We deduce that the Lord Chamberlain squelched the plan if it ever got so far as a formal proposal. The idea of augmenting opera house income by offering plays, however, continued to attract later proprietors, and in the 1770s the managers petitioned the Lord Chamberlain for the right to do so—without success.[17]

By about June 1764 Giardini was trying to placate his creditors and avoid arrest. The Chancery process, however, ground on regardless. The counter-suit filed by Mazziotti, et al., on 1 June comes as something of a surprise. The performers had a strong prima facie case, but the counter-suits are nonetheless remarkable because foreign nationals, unfamiliar with the labyrinthine processes of Chancery, rarely resorted to the law. Performers did not usually care to incur the huge legal fees 'which may possibly exceed the Value of the Matters in dispute'.[18] By bringing his own suit in the first place Giardini probably exacerbated his financial problems. According to *A Defence*, he had originally 'offered to submit the Matters in dispute

---

[16] A newspaper notice of 9 May denies that Manzuoli will fail to come the next season. Therefore, we judge the meeting to have occurred around the beginning of May 1764.

[17] See *The Correspondence of King George the Third from 1760 to December 1783*, 6 vols., ed. Sir John Fortescue (London: Macmillan, 1927-28), II, 191-194. This undated petition is printed with documents of 1770, but reference to competition from the Pantheon and its hiring Italian singers at extravagant salaries suggests a date *c*1775.

[18] *A Defence*, p. 6.

between him and all the other Parties, except Leone, to Arbitration', only to find that 'a certain Gentleman dissuaded these People from an Accommodation'.[19] We now know that Leone and the aggrieved performers were being supported, at first secretly, by Lieutenant-General Sir Robert Rich (1714-1785), an ex-soldier who had been seriously wounded at the Battle of Culloden. When Giardini discovered in late November 1764 that Rich was paying all their legal costs, he added the general to the list of defendants in Giardini v. Leone, et al.[20] Rich claimed purely altruistic motives: 'Considering the [other defendants] were Foreigners and Ignorant of the Laws and Language of this Country and unable through their Extream poverty to Assert their Innocence by a proper Defence he this Defendant from a mere Motive of Humanity and from a firm persuasion of the Justness of their Cause and from no other motive not only Supplied them with several Sums for their Immediate Support and Maintenance but also Undertook the Expence of their Defence in the Suit commenced against them.'[21]

Much of what we know about the last phase of the ruckus must be derived from R.P.'s obviously partisan *Defence of F. Giardini* (1765). (See Ill. 4.) This pamphlet is a direct reply to the *Réponse à un avertissement très-insolent*. Interestingly, the author alleges that the *Réponse*, though published in Leone's name (and the British Library copy is signed by him in MS on the title-page—see Ill. 5), was actually written by 'Cacophron' (that is, Discord), whose identity is made all but explicit by the bitterly ironic dedication of the *Defence* to L[ieutenan]t G[enera]l R[ich]:

It must be owned that you have carried the Art of Criticism, much higher in Music, than Longinus did the same Art, in Oratory and Poetry; and the World can never sufficiently admire your most accurate Judgement, in distinguishing, by the Difference of Stile, the Compositions of different Masters, and the Works of the same Masters, composed at different Times, and under different Dispositions of Mind, with so great a Nicety and Exactness, as to be able to determine not only who was the Author of any Piece of Music, but the Year, Day, and even the Hour, on which it was composed, the Humour in which the Author was when he composed it, and whether he then drank Small Beer, Porter, Burgundy, or Champaigne.

This mocking panegyric has a serious purpose. The writer of the pamphlet claims that Cacophron's antipathy for Giardini had its source in a musical incident. The violinist, after having drunk a pot of porter, 'was seized with a violent Estro Armonico; and in that

---
[19] *A Defence*, p. 6.
[20] C33/423, Decrees 1764A, Part 1, fols. 62 and 70 (28 November and 17 December 1764).
[21] C12/521/4 (answer of Rich), 12 February 1765.

Transport composed an English Catch'. Upon hearing it sung in company, Cacophron praised it and 'from several internal Marks, in the Harmony, Stile and Contrivance, pronounced it to be a famous Catch, composed by Maister Orlando Gibbons . . . after he had drank a Cup of Sack extraordinary, to the King's Health, on his Birth Day' (p. 14). Mortified and humiliated by his mistake, Cacophron (Rich) vowed to destroy Giardini.

A less colourful though more plausible reason for Rich's intervention on behalf of Leone and the beleaguered performers is easy to imagine. His actions have all the earmarks of a bid to gain control of the King's Theatre by buying up Giardini's debts and thereby becoming his principal creditor. While Rich denied having purchased the contracts of the defendants, he did admit to the following payments for 'Support and Maintenance': Mazziotti, £84 16s; Guglietti, £23 2s (plus other unspecified expenses); Marcucci, £5 5s; Baini, £40; Vento, £36. There is no accurate record of how much Giardini owed his performers at the end of the 1763-64 season, but the payment to Vento is close to the difference in salary between his first and second contracts. Rich may also have tried to assume liability for the unpaid salary of Carlo Graziani, the principal cellist in the opera house orchestra. In a long account appended to the *Réponse*, Graziani, formerly first cello in the private concerts sponsored by Le Riche de la Pouplinière at Passy, recounts how he was recruited in Paris with the promise of a guinea a night for playing in the King's Theatre band (see Appendix A, No. XXXVII). His engagement is confirmed by a letter of 12 August 1763, in which Giardini promised to write to Graziani and dismiss 'the Violincello of the Q[ueen]',[22] that is, John Gordon (Appendix A, No. XXV).[23] Giardini admitted that he owed Graziani money for services rendered (including 48 opera performances, two benefits and 18 subscription concerts), but not as much as the £60 18s claimed.

Ultimately, the Giardini lawsuits came to no conclusion: we have found no judgement in either case. Legal progress appears to have ground to a halt entirely when the litigants started to leave the country. Mazziotti departed for an engagement in Lisbon and for the 1765-66 season was joined there by Giuseppe Giustinelli, Angiola Sartori and Maddalena Tagnoni, who had apparently married the dancer Berardi.[24] The Court of Chancery was petitioned several times to examine material witnesses before they left England: for example, Gennaro Biasco Celestini, the Neapolitan fencing master who wit-

---

[22] This reading is implied by the original letter: 'Violoncello della R'.
[23] On 22 May 1764 Graziani and Giardini gave a joint concert in London; see *New Grove*, VII, 654, which does not record the cellist's engagement at the King's Theatre.
[24] See Manuel Carlos de Brito, *Opera in Portugal in the Eighteenth Century* (Cambridge: Cambridge University Press, 1989), p. 85.

nessed Vento's second contract,[25] and Regina Mingotti, who was heading for Germany at the beginning of July 1764.[26] And there was the further problem of translation, as very few of the parties concerned could read English: Leone, Mazziotti, Baini, Guglietti, Vento and Marcucci begged the Court's permission to swear their answers to Giardini's bill of complaint in Italian, because they 'do not understand the English Language'.[27] Of course, this could have been a stalling tactic. In fact, neither side had much to hope for. Giardini had no money for the singers to collect; nor could he gain much by proving conspiracy.

Conclusion

Giardini's letters illustrate just how dearly inexperience and misunderstanding could cost an opera company. His intentions were good: he hoped to hire a strong company, as his desire to engage Piccinni shows. While Piccinni never came to England, his *La buona figliuola* (first performed in London in 1766) was to become the most popular Italian opera of the second half of the eighteenth century at the King's Theatre.[28] But in 1763 Giardini wanted to mount *opera seria*, a form for which virtuoso singers were *sine qua non*. Satisfactory performers for *opera buffa* were vastly easier to find: given an attractive figure, an extrovert personality and a reasonable voice, a *buffo* could learn his trade—but *opera seria* depended upon heaven-sent, once-in-a-generation voices, and there were simply not enough of them.

As far as one can judge from scanty evidence, Giardini was paying modest but reasonable prices. Starting when he did, however, and given the King's Theatre's rather wobbly condition, he had little chance of recruiting good performers. When Leone reported that he could not find singers even of the quality of Sartori and Giustinelli (second-raters at the King's Theatre), the exasperated Giardini asked: 'I am to conclude then, that *all Music has deserted Italy* to turn *Stroller* in *Holland* and *Germany*' ('Bisogna dunque credere, che tutta la *Musica* è partita d'Italia ed è andata a far *villeggiatura* in *Germania* ed in *Olanda*'—Appendix A, No. XXVI). For a moment he forgot that he himself had left his native country to seek his fortune abroad.

Among other things, Giardini's instructions and letters tell us just what sort of 'fortune' might be made in London. We construct the following pay-scale from Appendix A, Nos. I, II, III, IV, V, VII and

---

[25] C33/421, Decrees 1763A, Part 2, fol. 252 (24 May 1764).
[26] Ibid., fol. 333 (29 June 1764).
[27] Ibid., fol. 329 (19 May 1764).
[28] Goldoni's libretto was based on Samuel Richardson's novel *Pamela*, an English connection that undoubtedly enhanced the opera's success. See W. C. Holmes, 'Pamela Transformed', *The Musical Quarterly*, 37 (1952), 581-594.

VIII, applying the 'Rule of Augmentation' to derive what Giardini considered a top salary for the category.

First Man	2000 zecchini	[£950]
First Woman	1600 zecchini	[£760]
if middling	1100 zecchini	[£552 10s]
Bass	650 zecchini	[£308 15s]
Tenor	550 zecchini	[£261 5s]
Two good Dancers	1300 zecchini	[£617 10s]
if middling	850 zecchini	[£403 15s]
Two promising young women	640 zecchini	[£304]
Composer (if Piccinni)		£200[29]
Vento [contract I]	300 zecchini	[£142 10s]

What Giardini paid for Giustinelli or Sartori, or for the three male dancers that he hired himself, is unknown. One cannot, therefore, construct a complete salary structure and obtain a total for the company. By Giardini's own testimony he was looking for a relatively cheap *primo uomo*: Mazziotti signed for 1500 zecchini (and actually for 1200), or only £712 10s (reduced to £570), but Luciani was asking £1500 and Guarducci £1000. There was probably some bargaining room in those figures, but in 1764-65 Manzuoli received £1500—and a banker guaranteed that it would actually be paid.[30]

Management arrangements for 1764-65 remained unsettled well into the autumn. Giardini clearly tried to hang onto at least a share in the opera concern, though ultimately without success. The struggle is reported in a series of letters in the Malmesbury correspondence. On 18 September 1764 Mrs Harris wrote 'nobody as yet can tell who is to have the management of the Opera', adding on the 29th 'they have not £1000 subscribed'.[31] As late as 19 October she commented that 'Giardini must go on, if he can, for none else can take it'. The next day, however, she reported a settlement. 'Now as to the state of operas, Giardini is gone quite away; so his partner, one Fermier, and

---

[29] Or 80 zecchini (£38) for one opera by mail (Appendix A, No. XXVI).
[30] *A Series of the Letters of the First Earl of Malmesbury . . . from 1745 to 1820*, ed. James Harris, Earl of Malmesbury, 2 vols. (London: R. Bentley, 1870), I, 113. The payment of the £1500 (and the guarantee) are proved in the Drummonds Bank accounts (Gibson, Appendix A). Orsi and Company were paid £30 (2%) for the guarantee. In a letter of February 1765 Leopold Mozart reports that 'Manzuoli is getting 1500 pounds sterling for this season and the money has had to be guaranteed in Italy as the previous impresario De Giardini went bankrupt last year'. *The Letters of Mozart and His Family*, ed. Emily Anderson, 3rd edn (New York: Norton, 1985), p. 54. This is nearly triple what Mazziotti was willing to accept.
[31] *A Series of the Letters of the First Earl of Malmesbury*, I, 111, 113. Following quotations from I, 115 and 116.

Crawford, will manage it. Manzolini [that is, Manzuoli] had made a vow never to sing what Bach had composed; but that quarrel is now made up, and Bach is to compose one opera; but what they are to do for hands, I cannot learn. I know almost all the old orchestra are engaged to the playhouses, and so are the dancers.' This is very interesting information: the editors of *The London Stage* were unaware of the identity of the managers for this season. Fermier is presumably the 'Mr. Farmer' mentioned by Giardini in letters XXI, XXIV and XXV (Appendix A).

J. C. Bach did indeed return with some success, and Vento was also retained as a house composer. None of Giardini's principals was re-engaged;[32] Manzuoli pleased the subscribers, as did Tenducci. There is some evidence that the Lord Chamberlain, Lord Gower, tried to intervene helpfully from behind the scenes. On 9 November 1764 Horace Walpole wrote to the British ambassador at Paris:

I write this by my Lord Chamberlain's order . . . You are desired by my Lord Gower, to apply to the Gentilhomme de la Chambre [the Duc le Fleury] for leave for Doberval the dancer, who was here last year, to return and dance at our opera forthwith. If the Court of France will comply with this request, we will send them a discharge in full, for the Canada bills and the ransom of their prisoners, and we will permit Monsieur D'Estain to command in the West Indies, whether we will or not.[33]

The performer desired was Jean Bercher Dauberval, a young dancer who had apparently been the principal attraction of Giardini's otherwise dismal 1763-64 season. These rather extraordinary political concessions were refused by the French Court because 'as the taste for music declines, the great expense of this *spectacle* makes it necessary to support it with dancing, which . . . is essential to a French opera'.[34] Even without Dauberval (who did not return to England until 1783), the company appears to have had a relatively successful season in 1764-65. Whether it was profitable is doubtful: a new management took over for 1765-66. We may wonder, though, how poor Giardini could be expected to recruit successfully with only his own meagre financial resources as inducement. So far as we are aware, the English government had been offering no concessions in international treaties on his behalf.

Giardini's troubles left behind some remarkable information about Italian opera in the mid-eighteenth century. On the whole, however, one suspects that he would have been wise to heed some

---

[32] Except Signora Cremonini, who had not actually joined the company in 1763-64, and Auretti (who had replaced Marcucci).
[33] *Horace Walpole's Correspondence*, XXXVIII, 460-461.
[34] *Horace Walpole's Correspondence*, XXXVIII, 483. Such deals to obtain favoured performers were not unknown between rulers on the Continent.

satiric advice published in the *Public Advertiser* of 3 June 1763, just as he was taking over from his predecessors.

Requisites necessary for those who would undertake to exhibit excellent Italian Operas in this renowned Metropolis; with the Consequences of such Undertaking. Submitted to the wise Heads of all future Managers.

  The Requisites are,

Money.	Ballet Master,
Time.	Money.
Money,	Dancers,
A Trip to Italy,	Money.
Money.	Scenes,
Singers,	Money.
Money.	Dresses,
Musical Composer.	Money.
Money.	Orchestra.
Poet,	Money.
Money.	Patience (not a little)
Painter,	Money *in sæcula seculorum*.
Money.	

The Consequences of such Undertakings to a Manager (after his enchanting the Town with four or five fine new Operas; which having been crowded for the two first Nights, the Singers would be left to warble to empty Benches; during the seven or eight succeeding ones) are.

Perplexity.	Imprisonment.
Disappointment.	Tatters.
Heart-breaking.	Madness
Poverty.	

  A Rope or Pistol; the last comfortable Resource of Italian Opera Managers.

Giardini did not resort to the rope or the pistol, and he apparently escaped madness, but on the evidence available he suffered his share of perplexity, disappointment, heartbreak, poverty and tatters—and imprisonment was a very near thing.

[26]

NAPOLI.

No. V.
Dopo aver sentito il *Monterati* e se *Luciani* sia preferibile a tutti gli altri, offerirgli ed estenderci alla somma di 1800 Zecchini. Se *Catalini* abbia voce forte, dar 1200 Zecchini, e se *Mazzanti* fin migliore 1400. Toccante la prima Donna, essendo veramente eccellente 1400.

No. VI.
Questo *Guadagni* non si sa se sia Soprano, Contralto, Tenore o Basso, per conseguenza non si puole decidere nulla sopra il suo articolo, eccetto un grandissimo caso di bisogno.

No. VII.
Prima Donna eccellente	Zecchini 1400
Se mediocre	1000
Primo uomo se *Luciani*	1800
Ballo	600
Coppia di *Ballerini* se buoni	1200
Se mediocri	800
Tenore	800
Ragazza d'aspettativa di buona voce e affetto per la coppia promesso	600

NB. Che ne' contratti eccetto il primo Soprano e prima Donna se sia necessità che non si debba spiegare il grado toccante gli altri. Nessuno alloggio nè spese di viaggio nè picciol vestiario, piuttosto qualche piccola cosa di più.

No. VIII. *Regola di aggiontamente in caso di bisogno.*
Sopra 1800 Zecchini fra il totale	Zecchini 200
Sopra le 1400 di più	200
Sopra le 1200	100
Sopra le 1000	100
Sopra le 600	50
Sopra le *Ragazze*, a ciascheduna	20
Sopra l' 800	50
Sopra le 500	50

No. IX. *Per i dieci Comandamenti.*

I. Non scoprir Segreto.
II. Non esser mai subitaneo.
III. Non trattar mai con Buffi.
IV. Civile con tutti.
V. Parlar poco ed ascoltar assai.
VI. Economia con Decenza.
VII. Ricordarsi di quello che si dice.
VIII. Aprire più orecchie che occhi.
IX. Chi serve un vero Amico obbliga se.
X. Le cose ardando bene ne avrai onore e profitto.

Formula

[27]

NAPLES.

No. V.
After having heard *Monterati*, if *Luciani* is preferable to all the rest, to offer him and to go as far as the Sum of 1800 Sequins. If *Catalini* has a strong Voice, to give 1200 Sequins, and if *Mazzanti* is better, 1400; touching the first Woman, if excellent, 1400.

No. VI.
This *Guadagni*, it is not known, whether he is a *Soprano*, a *Contralto*, a *Tenor*, or a *Bass*; consequently nothing can be decided on his account, except in case of extreme Necessity.

No. VII.
First Woman, excellent	1400 Zecchini
middling	1000
First Man, if *Luciani*	1800
Bass	600
A pair of Dancers, if good	1200
if middling	800
A Tenor	800
Two young Girls of Expectation, good Voices and handsome; for a couple I promise to forward their Capacities, and to pay	600

N. B. In the Contracts, unless to the first Soprano, and first Woman, (if necessary) not to explain the rank with respect to the rest.
To some Lodgings, expences of their Journey, or small cloathing, rather a trifle more.

No. VIII. *Rule of Augmentation in case of need.*
Upon 1800 Sequins upon the whole	200 Sequins.
Upon 1400	200
Upon 1200	100
Upon 1000	100
Upon 600	50
Upon the young *Tits*, to each	20
Upon 800	50
Upon 500	50

No. IX. *The Ten Commandments.*

I. To discover no Secrets.
II. Never to be hasty.
III. Not to treat with Buffos.
IV. To be civil to all.
V. To talk little, and hearken a great deal.
VI. Œconomy with Decorum.
VII. To remember what is said.
VIII. To open your Ears more than your Eyes.
IX. Who serves a true Friend, obliges himself.
X. When Things go well, you will have Honour and Profit.

Form

1. Sample pages from the *Réponse*; by permission of the Trustees of the British Library (see p. vi)

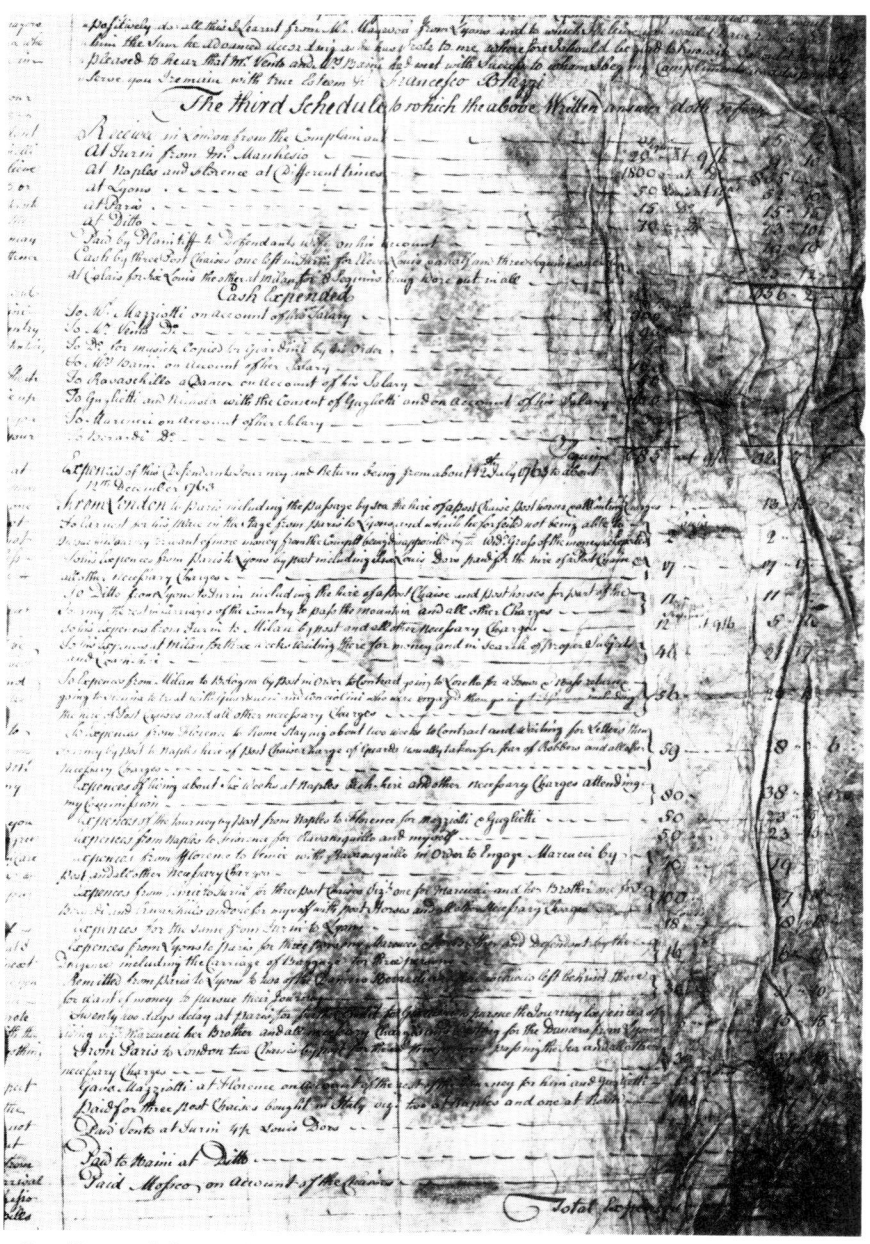

2. Part of Leone's itemized expenses: P.R.O. C12/517/16, Third Schedule; by permission of the Controller of Her Majesty's Stationery Office (see p. 19)

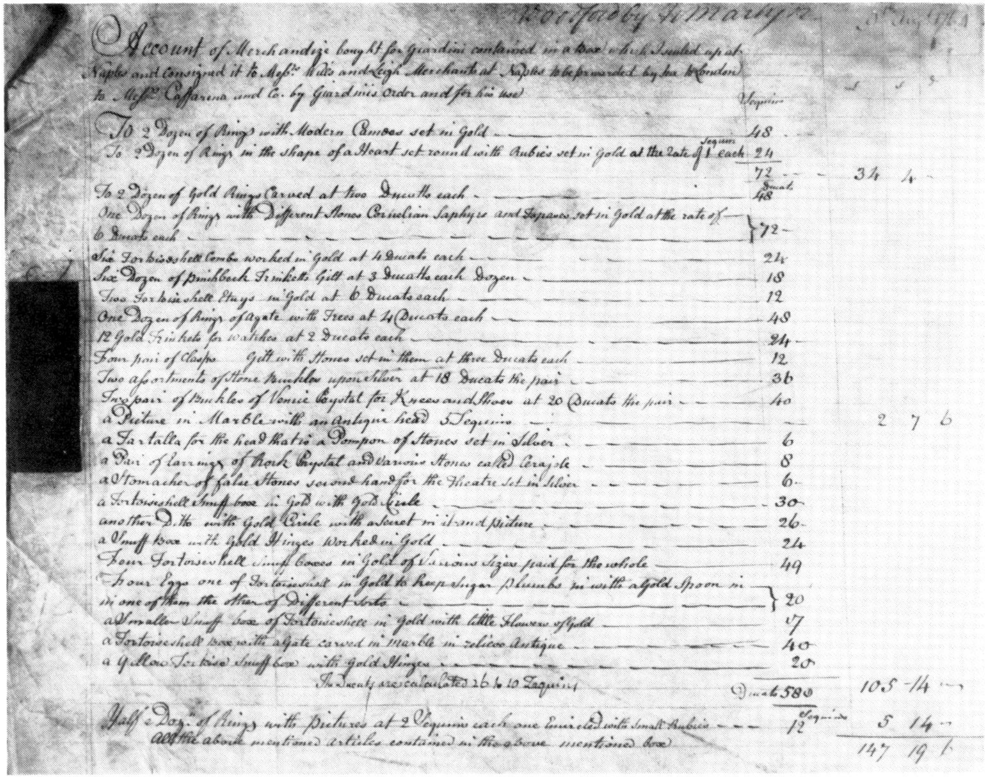

3. List of Goods purchased by Leone for Giardini: P.R.O. C12/517/16; by permission of the Controller of Her Majesty's Stationery Office (see p. 20)

A

DEFENCE

OF

F. GIARDINI,

FROM THE

Calumnies, Falshoods, and Misrepresentations,

OF

CACOPHRON,

In a PAMPHLET, published by him in the Name of

GABRIEL LEONE.

To which is subjoined,

A Short Account of the Cause of CACOPHRON's Resentment against GIARDINI.

LONDON:

Printed for R. DAVIS, in PICCADILLY, 1765.

4. *Defence* title-page; by permission of the Trustees of the British Library (see p. 24)

REPONSE
A UN
AVERTISSEMENT
TRES-INSOLENT,

Qui fut inféré dans une des Gazettes Publiques (le *Public Advertiser*) du 9me de May 1764. par FELICE GIARDINI, *Directeur de l'Opéra*, contre GABRIELE LEONE, *Agent* du dit GIARDINI.

On y a ajoûté
Les INSTRUCTIONS & les LETTRES de GIARDINI, pour mieux conftater la vérité.

Vedi, Leone, ch' io fo far il mio negozio.
Vous voyez bien, Leone, que je fais faire mes affaires.
Extr. d'une Lettre de Giardini, d. du 15. Juill. 1763. N. XXI.

ANSWER
To
A SCURRILOUS
ADVERTISEMENT
Publifhed
in the *Public Advertifer* of the 9th of May 1764.
By FELICE GIARDINI, *Director of the Opera*, againft GABRIEL LEONE, his late *Agent*.
To which are added
GIARDINI's INSTRUCTIONS and LETTERS.

"*You fee, Leone, I know how to do my own Bufinefs.*"
Vid. Giardini's Letter, July 15th 1763. N. XXI.

LONDON, 1764. *Gabriele Leone*

5. *Réponse* title-page; by permission of the Trustees of the British Library (see p. 24)

Appendix A

Giardini's Book of Instructions and Correspondence

Editorial note: Giardini's opera correspondence is found in two sources: *Réponse à un avertissement très-insolent* (1764) and Public Record Office C 12/517/16 (Leone's answer to Giardini's bill of complaint). So far as we are aware, the only extant copy of the *Réponse* is British Library 1347.e.10. The following is a conservatively corrected transcription of the documents, most of them as preserved in the *Réponse*, together with English translations taken from the same source.

Readers should be aware that the compositor who set the *Réponse* and the scribes who recorded the Chancery testimony were following Italian and French texts which they probably could not understand. The result is some disconcerting grammatical and orthographic quirks. We have silently corrected some of the most flagrant and misleading errors, have added accents whenever necessary for sense, and have silently extended some abbreviations in the Italian (e.g., 'sudo.' becomes 'sudetto') but otherwise have simply reproduced the texts as found. Original punctuation is retained throughout. Giardini was a Piedmontese, and his prose contains both Anglicisms and Gallicisms: to modernize would be virtually to rewrite. The translations in the *Réponse* are occasionally slanted to cast Giardini in a bad light, and attempt to expose his alleged dishonesty and incompetence by the use of capital letters and other typographical emphasis. They are, however, historical documents in their own right and are therefore likewise left unedited save for the correction of what are manifestly literals. A few self-evident items are not translated. Substantive textual variants among the main sources are given within brackets in the text itself. To save space, a few paragraphs have been run together in both the Italian and English versions. The numbering follows that in the *Réponse*. Letters and documents which are found only in the lawsuit are inserted in appropriate chronological position and given the number of their predecessor followed by a letter (e.g., No. XXVa). The translation of No. XXXVII (Graziani's affidavit) is our own since none is given in the *Réponse*.

Appendix A

As is typical of eighteenth-century Chancery bills and answers, C12/517/16 was written by legal scribes in brownish ink on large parchment membranes. This answer comprises seven membranes, varying in size from 930 x 750 mm. to 780 x 300 mm. Leone's main answer is written lengthwise across the entire membrane, while the various schedules appended thereto are given in three or four columns. Various stamps have been applied, and the membranes are held together by string. Each has at least one lacuna, but these were original features of the parchment which the scribes worked around.

Besides *Biographical Dictionary*, *New Grove*, Sartori, Wiel and *DEUMM*, the principal sources consulted in identifying singers and dancers mentioned in the documents are F. Florimo, *La scuola musicale di Napoli* (Naples, 1880); M. Rinaldi, *Due secoli di storia al Teatro Argentina* (Florence: Olschki, 1978); A. De Angelis, *Nella Roma papale: Il Teatro Alibert o delle Dame* (Tivoli, 1956).

Sources
A = *Réponse*: original language version
B = C12/517/16: original language version
C = *Réponse*: English translation
D = C12/517/16: English translation

ISTRUZIONI (Nos. I-XVIII)

No. I. Bisogna passare dal Signor *Brivio* [Giuseppe Ferdinando Brivio][1] e sentire il Signor *Cataneo*[2] e la sua scolara quella proposta da lui.[3] Toccante il Tenore, quando abbi buona voce, e buon personaggio scritturarlo al ritorno dal viaggio in caso di necessità e dopo d'aver ricevuto l'ultime decisive lettere dal Signor *Giardini*: circa l'onorario 500 e 50 Zecchini e che nel contratto non si parli di preferenza. Toccante la seconda Donna sua scolara non trovando altra per prima Donna meglio, al ritorno fare tutto il possibile di rompere il contratto, ancorchè costasse 1000 Zecchini, e regolarsi in conseguenza: Informarsi [B: informarti] a Milano se vi sia una buona coppia di Ballerini Groteschi: prendere l'ultimo spartito dell'Opere serie, ed informarsi circa un *Dies illa di Palladini*,[4] come pure *Vesperi* ed altro dove siano gran cori: e passare da Signor *Martini*[5] con complimento di *Giardini* detto *Piemontesino*, per lo stesso effetto.

[B adds: Padova. Essendomi proposto dal Signor Barretti[6] il posto di primo Musico nel Teatro Reale di Londra ed avendo pensato a tante spese che bisognano per transferirmi colà perciò dico che meno di 600 Chinee [sic] ed alloggio io non sarei in grado di servire quell' Impressa Io Francesco Rolfi.[7]

No. Ia. LETTERA di PROCURA fatta da Felice Giardini a Gabriel Leone.[8] A chi appartiene: Questo sia per certificare come che il proprietario della presente, Signor *Gabriel Leone*, si porta in Italia per contrattare a mio nome con quegli o quelle virtuose, come pure Ballerini o Ballerine, delle quali gliene ho dato le mie istruzioni. Segnato e suggellato di mio proprio pugno. Dato a Londra il dì 8 Luglio 1763. (L.S.) Felice Giardini.

No. II. PADOVA. Se in caso che a *Napoli* non si trovi meglio Musico soprano di *Rolfi*, il quale devi [B: devo] sentire prima di passare in Napoli, scritturarlo se sia possibile per la somma di 1200 Zecchini in tutto.

---

[1] See note 14 to Chapter 1, above.
[2] This is probably Antonio Cattaneo, who had sung in Scolari's *Statira* at Venice in 1756. See Wiel, p. 208.
[3] See No. VI, below.
[4] This is probably Giuseppe Paladino, maestro di cappella at the church of S. Sempliciano and teacher at the Collegio dei Nobili Longone. He taught Giardini and composed cantatas, oratorios and other sacred music for four to eight voices (see *DEUMM*, Le Biografie, V, 553).
[5] Despite the form of address (Signor), this is probably the famous Padre Giovanni Battista Martini (1706-1784), who was in Bologna at the time. See *New Grove*, XI, 723-725.

Appendix A

INSTRUCTIONS (Nos. I-XVIII)

No. I. You must go to Mr. *Brivio*'s, and hear Mr. *Cataneo* and his Scholar there, that was proposed by him. With respect to the *Tenor*, if he has a good Voice, and is of a good Figure, to contract with him on your return, in case of necessity, after having received the last decisive Letters [D: Decisive Orders] from Mr. *Giardini*. With respect to the Salary, 550 Sequins, and that in the Contract there be no mention made of preference. With regard to the second Woman his Scholar, not finding any other for first Woman, on your return to try all possible means to break the Contract, even if it should cost 1000 Sequins, and to regulate yourself accordingly: to inform yourself at Milan, if there is a good pair of comic Dancers: to take the last Score of the serious Operas, and to inform yourself of a *Dies illa* of *Palladini*, as also the *Vespers*, and others where there are *grand Chorusses*. To go to Sr. *Martini*, with compliments from *Giardini*, called *Piemontesino* for this purpose.

[D adds:] Padova It being proposed to Mr. Baretti to be first Singer in the Royal Theatre of London and having thought upon the Expences requisite to Transport him there for that reason I say that for Less than six hundred Guineas and Lodging I could not be in a way to serve that undertaking I Francisco Rolfi.[9]

No. Ia. LETTER OF ATTORNEY from Giardini to Leone. *To all whom it may concern.* This is to certify that the Proprietor of the present, Mr. *Gabriel Leone*, goes to Italy to contract in my Name with such Singers, Men and Women, and such Dancers, Men and Women, concerning whom I have given him my Instructions. Signed and sealed with my own Hand. Given at London the 8th of July 1763. (L.S.) Felice Giardini.

No. II. PADOUA. In case there is no better first Man Soprano [D: first musician Singer/soprano] at *Naples* than *Rolfi*, whom you must hear, before you go to *Naples*, to contract with him, if possible, for 1200 Sequins.

---

6   Probably Giuseppe (Joseph) Baretti, the London-based author of the *Account of the Manners and Customs of Italy* (London, 1769).
7   Rolfi appeared at the Teatro Argentina at Rome in 1748 and then at the S. Samuele and S. Moisè theatres at Venice in 1753.
8   Printed without number at the beginning of Giardini's instructions and letters in the *Réponse*. This letter is not found in C 12/517/16.
9   This passage is mistranslated. It should read: 'It being proposed *by* Mr. Baretti [that I] be first singer . . . and having thought about the expenses of transporting *me* there . . . I could not come for less than 600 guineas plus lodging . . . .'

The Impresario's Ten Commandments

No. III. ROMA. *Piccini* se viene alla primavera, 200 Lire Sterline facendo due Opere, occorrendo qualche arie di staccate [B: distacatte] oppure altro: e far delle diligenze per *Ballerini Groteschi* e per una voce di *Basso*: ed insiememente per qualche prima Donna oppure *altra d'aspettativa*.

No. IV. NAPOLI. Luciani[10] Soprano quale domanda £1500; Guarducci[11] Soprano quale domanda £1000; Catolini;[12] Mazziotti; Un Basso; Prima Donna; Ballerini Groteschi; Musica dell'ultima Opera come altra per cori e qualche ragazza d'aspettativa.

No. V. NAPOLI. Dopo aver sentitò il *Mentovati*[13] e se *Luciani* sia preferibile a tutti gli altri, offerirgli ed estendersi alla somma di 1800 Zecchini. *Catolini* e *Mazziotti*: Se *Catolini* abbia voce forte, dar 1200 Zecchini, e se *Mazziotti* sia migliore 1400. Toccante la prima Donna, essendo veramente eccellente 1400.

No. VI. Questo *Guadagnin*[14] non si sa se sia Soprano, Contralto, Tenore o Basso; per conseguenza non si puole decidere nulla sopra il suo articolo, eccetto un grandissimo caso di bisogno. [B adds:] Da Milano li 7 Giugno 1763: Il Signor Ferdinando Brivio propone il Signor Cataneo Tenore il quale richiede la somma di 300 Lire Sterl[ine] addossandosi delle spese.

No. VII. Prima Donna eccellente—*Zecchini* 1400; Se mediocre—1000; Primo uomo se *Luciani*—1800; Basso—600; Coppia di *Ballerini* se buoni—1200; se mediocri—800; Tenore—500; *Ragazze d'aspettativa* di buona voce e aspetto per la coppia prometto di avanzarle in Talento e paga—600. NB. Che ne' contratti eccetto il primo Soprano e prima Donna se sia necessità che non vi debba spiegare il grado toccante gli altri. Nessuno alloggio nè spese di viaggio nè picciol vestiario, piuttosto qualche piccola cosa di più.

---

[10] Domenico Luciani, actually a tenor, who sang mainly serious roles, appeared at the Teatro Argentina, Rome, in 1759, at the Teatro S. Carlo, Naples, in 1762 and again at the Argentina in 1763. He went to London and performed at the King's Theatre, Haymarket, in the season of 1768-69. See *Biographical Dictionary*, IX, 378.

[11] Tommaso Guarducci, a castrato (b. Montefiascone, Viterbo, c1720; d. after 1770). A pupil of Bernacchi at Bologna, he was summoned to Madrid by Farinelli in 1750 and remained there on and off for 20 years. He also sang at the Vienna Burgtheater in 1755, at the Teatro Ducale, Milan, in 1758, at the Teatro S. Carlo, Naples, in 1758-59 and at the Teatro Argentina, Rome, in 1765. He served as *primo uomo* at the King's Theatre, Haymarket, in 1766-67 and remained in London until 1769. Burney gave him high praise. See *Biographical Dictionary*, VI, 438-440. In 1770 he returned to Rome, where he appeared in Piccinni's *Didone abbandonata* at the Argentina (*DEUMM*, Le Biografie, III, 348).

Appendix A

No. III. ROME. If *Piccini* comes in the Spring, 200 £. [for] making two Operas, adapting some Staccato Airs[15] or others—to use Diligence for *comic Dancers*, and for a *Bass*, likewise for a first Woman-Singer, or *one of Expectation*.

No. IV. NAPLES. *Lucciani*, a Soprano, who asks 1500 £; *Guarducci* who asks 1000 £; *Catolini*; *Mazziotti*; A Bass; First Woman; Comic Dancers; The Score [D: Musick] of the last Opera, and *some for Chorusses*, and a young Girl of Expectation.

No. V. NAPLES. After having heard *Mentovati* [*recte*: those already mentioned], if *Lucciani* is preferable to all the rest, to offer him and to go as far as the Sum of 1800 Sequins. *Catolini* and *Mazziotti*; if *Catolini* has a strong Voice, to give 1200 Sequins, and if *Mazziotti* is better, 1400; touching the first Woman, if excellent, 1400.

No. VI. This *Guadagnin* [D: Guadognin], it is not known, whether he is a *Soprano*, a *Contralto*, a *Tenor*, or a *Bass*; consequently nothing can be decided on his account, except in case of extreme Necessity. [D adds:] From Milan 7th June 1763 Mr. Ferdinand Brivio proposes Mr. Cataneo Tenor who asks the sum of £300 sterling paying his Expences.

No. VII. First Woman, excellent—1400 *Zecchini*; middling—1000; First Man, if *Lucciani*—1800; Bass—600; A pair of Dancers, if good—1200, middling—800; A Tenor—500; *Two young Girls of Expectation, good Voices and handsome* [D: good voice and face]; for a couple I promise to forward their Capacities [D: to Advance them in their Talent], and to pay 600. *N.B.* In the Contracts, unless to the first Soprano, and first Woman, (if necessary) not to explain [D: not to specify] the rank with respect to the rest. To none Lodging, expences of their Journey, or small cloathing, rather a trifle more.

---

[12] This may be Giacomo Cattilini (or Catilini), a Roman singer and *ultima parte* at the Teatro S. Cassiano, Venice, in 1742-43, at Florence in 1745-46, and at the Teatro Argentina in Rome in 1747. See Robert Lamar Weaver and Norma Wright Weaver, *A Chronology of Music in the Florentine Theater 1590-1750* (Detroit: Information Coordinators, 1978), and Wiel, pp. 137-138, 145.
[13] Clearly a misreading of 'i mentovati' (i.e., 'those mentioned').
[14] Clearly not Gaetano Guadagni (c1725-1792), who had performed in London between 1748 and 1755 (*Biographical Dictionary*, VI, 435-438). John Rosselli suggests that 'Guadagnin' is probably a Venetian nickname for a pupil or imitator of Guadagni. The reference could be to Giovanni Battista Guadagnini, who sang in four operas at S. Moisè in 1761-62, including Piccinni's *L'astrologa*. See Wiel, p. 233.
[15] This mistranslation of 'separate' or 'detached' arias in C is also found in D.

The Impresario's Ten Commandments

No. VIII. *Regola di aggiunzione in caso di bisogno*

Sopra 1800 Zecchini fra il totale		*Zecchini* 200
Sopra le 1400	" di più	200
Sopra le 1200	" più	100
Sopra le 1000	"	100
Sopra le 600	"	50
Sopra le *Ragazze* [B: Raggazzi], a ciascheduna		20
Sopra l' 800		50
Sopra le 500		50

No. IX. *Per i dieci Comandamenti*
  I. NON SCOPRIR SEGRETO.
  II. NON ESSER MAI SUBITANEO.
  III. NON TRATTAR MAI CON BUFFI.
  IV. CIVILE CON TUTTI.
  V. PARLAR POCO ED ASCOLTAR ASSAI.
  VI. ECONOMIA CON DECENZA.
  VII. RICORDARSI DI QUELLO CHE SI DICE.
  VIII. APRIRE PIÙ ORECCHIE CHE OCCHI.
  IX. CHI SERVE UN VERO AMICO OBBLIGA SE.
  X. LE COSE ANDANDO BENE NE AVRAI ONORE E PROFITTO.

No. X. *Formola di Contratto*
In Dei Nomine, Amen. Londra &c. Per la presente privata scrittura da valere ed aver tenere, come se fosse un pubblico giurato Istromento apparisca qualmente (nome) si obbliga di ritrovarsi in Londra per la metà di Settembre 1763, ed ivi trattenersi fino a tutto il mese di Giugno 1764, e durante detto tempo intervenire e cantare a tutte e quante quelle prove e recite dell'Opere (*), che si faranno nel Teatro Reale, e che le saranno ordinate dal Signor Felice Giardini Direttore di detta Opera: Dippiù si obliga il suddetto (nome) di non cantare in veruna Assemblea o Concerto o altro luogo fuori dell'Opera senza prima averne ottenuta la permissione in scritto dal detto Signor Giardini, e mediante le suddette condizioni il suddetto Felice Giardini s'obbliga di pagare al suddetto (nome) per le sue virtuose fatiche Zecchini — o loro valuta in tutto e per tutto in due rate, le metà dopo le venticinque recite ed il rimanente alla fine della stagione, intendendosi che ne' casi d'incendio di Teatro, divieto pubblico e simili, il suddetto — debba essere pagato a proporzione delle recite e come si costuma in Italia [B: ne Teatri d'Italia] in simili congiunture, e finalmente li suddetti Felice Giardini e (nome) concordemente e di reciproco consenso convengono che quello di loro che contravverrà una o più volte ad uno o più degli articoli di sopra accordati pagherà

Appendix A

No. VIII. *Rule of Augmentation in case of need*
Upon 1800 Sequins upon the whole	Sequins 200
Upon 1400	200
Upon 1200	100
Upon 1000	100
Upon 600	50
Upon the young *Tits*, to each	20
Upon 800	50
Upon 500	50

No. IX. *The Ten Commandments*
I. TO DISCOVER NO SECRETS.
II. NEVER TO BE HASTY.
III. NOT TO TREAT WITH BUFFOS.
IV. TO BE CIVIL TO ALL.
V. TO TALK LITTLE, AND HEARKEN A GREAT DEAL.
VI. ŒCONOMY WITH DECORUM.
VII. TO REMEMBER WHAT IS SAID.
VIII. TO OPEN YOUR EARS MORE THAN YOUR EYES.
IX. WHO SERVES A TRUE FRIEND, OBLIGES HIMSELF.
X. WHEN THINGS GO WELL, YOU WILL HAVE HONOUR AND PROFIT.

No. X. *Form of a Contract.*
In the Name of God, Amen. By this private [D: present] writing of value and tenour, as if it was a sworn Instrument, it appears, that _____ obliges ____self to be in England [D: London] by the middle of September 1763, and to remain there to the very end of June 1764, and to come and sing at all and every Rehearsal of such Operas (*) as shall be performed in the Royal Theatre, and which shall be appointed by Mr. FELICE GIARDINI, Manager [D: undertaker] of the said Opera, moreover obliges ____ self the said _____ not to sing in any Assembly or Concert or other place, except at the Opera, without having first obtained permission in writing from the said GIARDINI, and on these conditions the said Mr. FELICE GIARDINI obliges himself to pay to the said _____ for his (or her) trouble and fatigue Sequins _____ or their value in full every where in two proportions. The half after twenty-five representations, and the other half at the end of the season. It being understood that in case of the Theatre's being on fire, a public prohibition or the like, the said _____ shall be paid in proportion to the representations, as is usual in Italy in the like cases. And finally, the said FELICE GIARDINI and _____ do by mutual consent reciprocally agree, that which ever of them shall fail once or oftener in the above articles agreed on, shall pay to the other the sum of _____ over

all'altro ogni volta e per ciascheduna contravenzione la pena di (somma) oltre al rifacimento de' danni; le quali pene e danni dovranno essere computati in conto di paga. In fede di che questa con altra simile sarà segnata da ambe le parti.

  Testimonio   Jo. Gabriele Leone
                     per Felice Giardini

(*) e altri Trattenimenti Musicali.

No. XI. La penalità che debba essere sempre il quarto della paga [B: il quarto parte dell'onorario provisto (previsto?) che del Canto loro ne diano]. I pagamenti saranno alla loro disposizione cioé in 2, o 3, o 4 rate.[16] L'avanzo del denaro che non debba eccedere la quarta parte dell' Onorario, con questo che dal canto loro ne diano securità di rendersi a Londra.

No. XII. Se in caso *Piccini* non accettasse e che non potesse venire, prendere questo *Mattia Vento* non eccedendo però la paga di 220 Zecchini; con l'articolo nel contratto che debba obbligarsi a mettere assieme pasticci, comporre arie duetti fare recitativi secondo che gli verrà ordinato dal Signor *Felice Giardini*.

No. XIII. Ricordarsi che contrattando con qualsi sia persona che non abbia compiuto i 21 anni di far contratto anche col Padre o Madre o Parenti o Maestro.

No. XIV. Mesdames La Veuve *Grasse & Huet* a Paris; *Giuseppe Marchisio* a Torino; Il Signor Abbate *Prasca* a Milano; Signor *Agostino Domenico Varese* a Genova; Il Signor *Giuseppe Morris* a Roma; Signor *Matteo Chamberont* e *Figlio* [B: figlii] a Napoli.

No. XV. *Consolini*[17] —600 *Zecchini*; in Siena cinquanta o cento di più.[18]

No. XVI. Se un buon Castrato—400 Zecchini.
La *Brucciatina*[19] a Venezia.
La *Baglioni*[20] in Fiorenza.
I *Varanelli*[21] Groteschi in Fiorenza.

---

[16] C12/517/16 omits this sentence.
[17] Not otherwise known to us, although this might be Tommaso Consoli (or Consol), a male soprano now known for having sung in the first performance of Mozart's *La finta giardiniera* in the role of Ramiro (Munich, 1775) and in *Il re pastore* (Salzburg, 1775), probably in the role of Elisa. In 1778-79 he sang at Venice in the Teatro S. Benedetto, in 1780 at Rome at the Argentina, and in 1781-82 at the Teatro S. Carlo, Naples. See Pierluigi Petrobelli, 'Il Re Pastore una serenata', in *Mozart-Jahrbuch* (1984-85), 109-114.
[18] The Italian version, which means literally that Consolini received 50 or 100 zecchini

Appendix A

and above the reparation of damages, the which forfeits and damages shall be reckoned on account of pay. In testimony of which this with a Duplicate shall be signed by both parties.

I GABRIEL LEONE, *for* FELICE GIARDINI.

(*) Or other Musical Entertainments.

No. XI. The penalty should be always the fourth part of the pay. The payments shall be at their own dispositions, that is in 2, 3, or 4 parts. The advance of money ought not to exceed the fourth part of their pay, provided they give security to repair to London to sing there.

No. XII. In case *Piccini* should not accept or could not come, to take this *Mattia Vento*, not exceeding the price of 220 Sequins; with an article in his Contract, that he shall be obliged to put Pasticcio's [D: Pasticcios (medley Operas)] together to compose airs, duets [D: two airs], recitative, as shall be directed him by Mr. *F.G.*

No. XIII. To remember in contracting with any persons under 21 years, to contract also with the Father, Mother, Relations, or Master.

No. XIV. Mesdames the Widow *Grass* and *Huet* at Paris. *Giuseppe Marchesio* at Turin. The Abbey Prasca *at Milan. Agostino Domenico Varese* at Genoa. Mr. *Giuseppe Morris* at Rome. Mr. *Matteo Chamberont* and *Sons* at Naples.

No. XV. *Consolini* in Siena—600 *Sequins*. Fifty or one hundred more.

No. XVI. If a good Castrato—400 Sequins.
The *Brucciatina* at Venice.
Baglioni in Florence.
The *Varanelli's* Comic Dancers at Florence.

more in Siena, seems to be garbled. The English translation better conveys the sense that Leone was allowed to apply the Rule of Augmentation.

[19] Clementina Spagnioli (see No. XXVIIb, below). She appeared at the Teatro S. Samuele at Venice in 1752-53, at the Teatro S. Benedetto, Venice, in 1757, at the Teatro S. Carlo, Naples, in 1761-62 (in J. C. Bach's *Alessandro nell'Indie*). She joined the King's Theatre for the 1765-66 season, and in 1770 she was at the Teatro Comunale, Bologna.

[20] Probably one of the elder daughters of Francesco Baglioni. See *New Grove*, II, 17-18.

[21] Not otherwise known to us.

No. XVII. Non trovandosi una buona prima Donna cercato di avere la *Brucciatina* Spagnioletta [B: Spagnioli] ed il prezzo di 1400 Zecchini insino ai mille ed ottocento.

No. XVIII. Informarsi d'un certo *Consolini* Castrato soprano che deve avere buona voce, il quale ha cantato a *Venezia* all'Ascensa. Londra 12 Luglio 1763: Ricevuto dal Signor *Giardini—quindici Guinee*; [B adds:] Riceuto dal Signor Giardini venti Zecchini per mano del Signor Marchisio a Turino; Riceuto quindeci luigi dal Signor Maurò.

LETTERE di Felice Giardini

No. XIX. Giardini to the Widow Grasse et Huet at Paris, 14 June 1763.
Madame, Par mon Ami, Monsieur *Caffarena*,[22] j'ai reçu vôtre lettre du 30 passé. Je vous remercie de vos offres & de la bonne volonté que vous me faites paroître en vous intéressant à faire mes commissions. Le Tailleur de l'Opéra[23] partira d'ici Vendredi prochain pour se rendre à Paris; il ne manquera pas de passer chez vous; il a toutes mes instructions, & vous pourrés [B: pourai], Madame, lui fournir ce qu'il demande, en tenant un juste accompte qui puisse se confronter avec le sien.

Vous recevrez [B: recevarais] celle-ci par Monsieur *Leone*, qui passe à Paris pour se rendre en Italie pour me conduire les Chanteurs & Chanteuses que j'ai engagés. Je vous prie de lui faire l'avance de 300 Livres de France, & de le tirer sur moi en vous faisant donner un double Reçu de la même date.

Je ne manquerai pas de mon côté de vous marquer ma reconnoissance en vous recommandant tous ces *Seigneurs & Dames Angloises* de ma connoissance qui se rendront à Paris. En attendant je vous prie de me croire avec beaucoup de consideration. Vôtre très-humble & très-obeïssant Serviteur Felice Giardini.

No. XX. Giardini to Leone, 12 July 1763.
Amico Carissimo, In questo punto vengo di ricevere nuove da Venezia come che questo Signor *Rolfi* sia piuttosto indifferente, anzi cattivo, così che fate tutti gli sforzi per l'altro primo uomo, e fra l'altre cose questo *Consolini*. Di prime Donne, *Brivio* mi scrive che vi è una certa *Bianchi*[24] che non è cattiva, procurate di sentirla. Il vostro

---

[22] Caffarena and Morris, evidently Roman merchants with offices in London.
[23] Probably Joseph Capitani; see No. XXXVII.
[24] Probably Marianna Bianchi [Tozzi], who had sung as *ultima parte* with Colomba Mattei at Reggio Emilia in 1754; in 1757 at the Teatro S. Salvatore, Venice; in 1759 at the Teatro S. Moisè, Venice (with Manzuoli), including a performance of Mattia Vento's *L'Egiziana*. In 1764 she was to sing at the Teatro S. Cassiano, Venice; in 1770-71 at the

Appendix A

No. XVII. Not finding a good first Woman, try to get the *Brucciatina Spagnioletta*, the price 1400 Sequins up to 1800.

No. XVIII. To inform yourself of a certain *Consolini* Castrato Soprano [D: gelding soprano], who should have a good voice, and sung at Venice at the Assumption. London July 12, 1763. Receiv'd of Mr. *Giardini* £15 15s 0d. [D adds:] Received of Mr. Giardini by the hands of Mr. Marchesio at Turin Twenty Sequins; Received 15 Louis of Monsr. Mauro.

LETTERS of Felice Giardini

No. XIX.
Madam, By my friend Mr. *Caffarena* I have received your Letter of the 13 [D: 30th Ulto] instant. I am obliged to you for the interest you take in my commissions. The Opera-Taylor sets out for Paris next Friday, and will wait upon you. He has my Instructions, and you may furnish him with what he may have occasion for, keeping an account that may tally with his.

You will receive this from Mr. *Leone*, who takes Paris in his way to Italy, in order to bring me the Singers, whom I have engaged. I desire you will advance him 300 French Livres, and draw on me for that Sum, taking a double Receipt of the same date.

As a proof of my gratitude, I shall not fail to recommend you to all the *Lords* and *Ladies of my acquaintance*, who go to Paris. In the mean time, believe me with great consideration &c. Felice Giardini.

No. XX.
Dearest Friend, I Have just received news from Italy [D: from Venice], that this Mr. *Rolfi* is indifferent, not to say bad; do all you can then for the other first Man, and among other things, this *Consolini*. With regard to a first Woman, *Brivio* writes me word, there is a certain *Bianchi*, who is not bad; endeavour to hear her. Your Son is a little

Teatro S. Carlo, Naples, and also at the Teatro Comunale, Bologna, as Euridice in Gluck's *Orfeo*.

figlio sta un poco meglio, ma domani gli condurrò *Bromfeild* [sic] il quale ne avrà tutta quella cura come se fosse un Principe del sangue. *Giustinelli*[25] piange amaramente la sua coglioneria. La *Cremonini*[26] mi ha mandato a ricercare più di sette volte ma senza prò: NON CONOSCONO GIARDINI. La lettera di Todi[27] l'ho fatta leggere a Sodi[28] ed a Noferi,[29] i quali mi hanno rotto tutti i scagni a forza di buttarsi di quà e di là dalle gran risa. Io gliela rimanderò, come vi ho detto, e si spera che questa maniera ci procurerà la continuazione de' suoi caratteri, la qual cosa non ci terrà malinconici. Ricordati dell'amico, *leggi i commandamenti* non sparagniare fatica per l'amico, che l'amico non ne sparagnierà per te: Addio di tutto cuore sono Felice Giardini. Londra al dì 12 Luglio cioè Martedi 1763.

Venerdi scriverò e la mia sarà diretta all'Abbate *Prasca* a Milano.

No. XXI. Giardini to Leone, 15 July 1763.
Amico Carissimo, Alla fine il *Giustinelli* mi è venuto a lagrimare tanto che l'ho preso, ma col *Ribasso di cinquanta Zecchini*, e la medesima cosa ho fatto alla *Cremonini*, la quale fu obbligata di raccomandarsi alla Sartori;[30] così che se senti a parlare di questo second'uomo, che ha cantato a Padova ultimamente con *Elisi*,[31] potrai trattarlo per un altr'anno. VEDI, LEONE, CH'IO SO FARE IL MIO NEGOZIO: procura di fare presto, e sopra tutto i ballerini. Ben presto riceverò l'ultima decisiva di *Romani*,[32] che se caso mai facesse che non mi rimandasse il contratto in dietro, subito il tempo spirato allora ti dirò che cosa bisogna fare, adesso mando a vedere come stanno in casa la tua moglie e figli, e finirò la mia lettera dopo. L'altre poste le invierò tutte a *Napoli*, e spero che le giungerai nell'istesso tempo.

Il mio servo mi vien di dire che la tua moglie sta bene e che ti ha scritto. Il ragazzo non è guarito, ma il Chirurgo lo dice fuori di pericolo. *Todi* assassina la *Sartori* con lettere di condoglienza [condoglianza] e di miseria: s'aspetta ben presto quà; con tutto ciò gli manderò la sua lettera. *Trombetta*, la *Mattei* e *Bach* sono partiti oggi

---

[25] Giuseppe Giustinelli, a castrato from Orvietto; he sang at Rome from 1758 to 1761 at the Argentina and Alibert theatres as *prima parte* in serious operas. He joined the King's Theatre company in February 1763 and worked at Drury Lane in 1764-65. See *Biographical Dictionary*, VI, 229.

[26] Clementina Cremonini sang at the King's Theatre in the spring of 1763 and at Drury Lane in 1763-64. She performed with the seven-year-old Mozart at Spring Garden on 5 June 1764. See *Biographical Dictionary*, IV, 37-38.

[27] Not otherwise known to us.

[28] Pietro Sodi (c1716-c1775), ballet master for Giardini at the King's Theatre in 1763-64. He was a dancer and choreographer of some distinction who had been *maître de ballet* at the Comédie Italienne 1753-1756 and 1758-1760. He first performed in London at Covent Garden in 1761. See *New Grove*, XVII, 440-441.

[29] Giovanni Battista Noferi (c1740-1782), violinist and composer. He specialized in

Appendix A

better, but to-morrow I shall take *Bromfield* to him, who will be as careful of him, as if he was a Prince of the Blood. *Giustinelli* laments his folly bitterly. The *Cremonini* has sent for me several times [D: more than seven times], but to no purpose: THEY DO NOT KNOW GIARDINI. I have read Todi's Letter to Noferi and Sodi, who have shook all my chairs to pieces with laughing. I will return it to him, as I told you, in hopes that this will procure us a continuation of his correspondence, which will preserve us from melancholy. Remember your friend. *Read the Commandments*. Spare no pains for your friend, as your friend will spare none for you. Adieu, I am cordially Felice Giardini. London, July 12, that is Tuesday, 1763.

I will write by Friday's post, & direct my Letter to the Abbey *Prasca* at Milan.

No. XXI.

Dearest Friend, At last *Giustinelli*'s lamentations [D: Giustinelli has been with me crying so] have induced me to engage him, but with *an abatement of 50 Sequins*: and at the recommendation of the Sartori, I have accepted the *Cremonini*, and on the same terms: so that if you should hear of a certain second Man Singer, who sung latterly at Padua with *Elisi*, you may treat with him for another year. YOU SEE, LEONE, I KNOW HOW TO DO MY OWN BUSINESS. Make haste, and above all for the *Dancers*. I am in constant expectation of *Romani*'s final answer; if he does not return me the contract, as soon as ever the time is expired, I will tell you what to do. I am now sending to enquire after your Wife and Family, and will conclude my Letter afterwards. I shall for the future direct my Letters at Naples, where I hope they will find you.

My Servant brings me word your Wife is well, and has wrote to you. Your Son is not yet recovered; but the Surgeon declares him out of danger. *Todi* torments the *Sartori* with Letters of condolence and misery; he is expected here: with all this I shall send him his Letters. *Trombetta*, *Mattei*, and *Bach* are set out this day for Paris—great

---

dance music, and late in his life served as orchestra leader for ballet at the King's Theatre, Haymarket. See *Biographical Dictionary*, XI, 39-40, and *New Grove*, XIII, 262-263.

[30] Angiola Sartori sang often at S. Cassiano, S. Angelo and S. Salvatore at Venice from 1749 to 1761. She had performed at the King's Theatre, Haymarket, in 1761-62. See *Biographical Dictionary*, XIII, 209-210.

[31] Filippo Elisi, a Roman castrato, sang at the Teatro S. Samuele, Venice, in 1739-40, at Rome alternately at the Argentina and Alibert theatres from 1741 to 1744, at the Teatro S. Giovanni Grisostomo, Venice, in 1745-46, returning to the Argentina in 1747-48, 1752-53 and again in 1763. He sang at the King's Theatre, Haymarket, in 1760-61. He performed at the Teatro S. Benedetto, Venice, in 1764-65, and returned to London for 1765-66, said to have lost his voice and grown fat as a porpoise. See *Biographical Dictionary*, V, 48.

[32] Not otherwise known to us.

per Parigi: Grandissimi pianti, ma che si potevano asciugare senza gran fazzoletto. La *Sartori* parte Mercordì prossimo per Parigi, PARLANDO CON CREANZA. *Noferi* vi saluta. Adesso sanno tutti che tu sei partito per l'Italia, e sono stupefatti: chi dice che è una coglioneria, e chi dice che non è vero; e secondo il solito fanno i loro almanacchi sopra nissun fondamento.

Mr. *Farmer*[33] ha pranzato quà: abbiamo bevuto alla tua salute; così conservala secondo la nostra intenzione, fà pulito e ricordati che sono di tutto il cuore tuo Felice Giardini. Londra al 15 Luglio 1763.

No. XXII. Giardini to Leone, 21 July 1763.

Amico Carissimo, Oggi vengo di ricevere la *confermazione* di *Romani Tenore famosissimo* al servizio del Re di Prussia *con la sua scrittura*, cosicchè *del Tenore non ne parliamo più*: ho scritturato *Giustinelli* e la *Cremonini*, e la *Sartori* come vi dissi nell'ultima mia; così che mi bisogna il *prim'Uomo* la *prima Donna* ed il *Basso*, queste *Ragazze* e *Ballerini*: A te *Gabriele* fatti onore che ne sarai [sarei] contento. Abbiamo rimandata la lettera di *Todi* a lui stesso ed *Agos*[34] gli ha scritto che *Caruso*[35] era arrivato quì con la sua moglie, e che loggiava in casa sua infino al suo ritorno di Scozia; Oltre di ciò tutti quelli i quali sono stati complimentati da lui, gli hanno scritto una lettera lunghissima congratulandosi seco del suo buon successo; così che riceverà un pacchetto di 22 Scellini di lettere. Questo giunto alla Gelosia ed alla nobilissima miseria che gode in quel paese si spera che lo farà correr a Londra a piedi. L'invenzione di questo è del famoso *Agos*. La tua moglie e figlio si portano bene, e subito che potrò decentemente andarci in casa, non mancherò di portarmi in persona per sapere delle sue nuove.

—AVANTI IERI IN CITTÀ, HO SENTITO A DIRE DA MOLTI CHE QUESTO MAZZIOTTI E GUARDUCCI SIANO VERAMENTE I MIGLIORI SOGGETTI, E QUESTA BRUCCIATINA LA MEGLIO PRIMA DONNA. ORA SE POSSO AVERE QUESTI ANCORCHE SIANO CARI, CIOÈ QUALCHE CENTO ZECCHINI DI PIÙ DEL NOSTRO MANIPOLO NON IMPORTA. Allora prendi il resto che sia bello ed a buon mercato: Intendi bene questo bilancio. Leva dal cavolo per dare al broccolo: Se non puoi aver broccolo, scegli buoni cavoli. Addio, sto anzioso delle lettere e mi dico tutto tuo Felice Giardini. Londra 21 Luglio 1763.

Se puoi ritrovare in Napoli *cassette di Fiori* di penna[36] di tutte le sorti grandi e piccioli, che sono fatte dalle monache; spediscele alla direzione di Caffarena con polizza di carico.

---

[33] Not otherwise known to us; see reference to Mr Fermier above, p. 28.
[34] This may be the shadowy violinist Joseph Agus (fl. 1763) recorded in the *Biographical Dictionary*, I, 43. As Giuseppe Agus he is identified in *New Grove*, I, 170, as a composer of ballet music for the opera (c1725-c1800).
[35] Unidentified, unless this is the cellist Caruso (fl. 1748-1756) recorded in the *Biographical Dictionary*, III, 93.

regrets and lamentations, but easily shaken off [D: dried up without a great handkerchief]. Sartori (TO SPEAK WITH RESPECT) goes next Wednesday to Paris. *Noferi* salutes you. Your being gone to Italy is now known, and causes much surprize. Some say, it is a Hum-bug; others, that it is not true; and all draw conclusions, according to custom, without any foundation.

Mr. *Farmer* dined here, we drank your health. Take care of it for our sake. Act well, and remember that I am cordially Yours, Felice Giardini. London, July 15, 1763.

No. XXII.

Dearest Friend, *Romani, the famous Tenor* in the King of Prussia's service, is this Day *confirmed* to me, and *I have his Contract*, so that we *need think no more about a Tenor*. I have engaged *Giustinelli*, the *Cremoni*, and the *Sartori*, as I told you in my last. I want then a *first Man Singer*, a *Bass*, and first Woman Singer: the *Girls* and the *Dancers*. Do honour to yourself, *Gabriel*, by satisfying me. We have returned *Todi*'s Letter to him, and *Agos* has wrote to him, that *Caruso* is arrived with his Wife, and lodged in his house since his return from Scotland, and by way of addition, all who have been complimented by him, have wrote him congratulatory Letters on his good success, so that he will receive a packet of Letters, which will cost him 22 Shillings; this added to his jealousy, and the extreme misery he suffers in that Country, will, it is to be hoped, induce him to run bare-foot to London. This invention [D: mention] is the work of the famous *Agos*. Your Wife and Son are well. I will go and see them as soon as I can with propriety.

—THE DAY BEFORE YESTERDAY I WAS INFORMED BY MANY IN THE CITY, THAT THIS MAZZIOTTI AND GUARDUCCI ARE REALLY THE BEST SINGERS, AND THE BRUCCIATINA THE BEST WOMAN SINGER; IF THEN I CAN GET THESE, ALTHO' THEY SHOULD BE DEARER THAN THE PRICES WE FIXED ON, (THAT IS SOME HUNDRED SEQUINS MORE) NO MATTER. In that case procure the rest, as cheap and good as you can. Weigh well the following maxim: Take from the worst to give to the best. And if you cannot get the latter, chuse among the former [D: take from the Cabbages to give to the sprouts and if you Cannot get good sprouts chuse the best Cabbages]. Adieu, I am anxious for your Letters &c. cordially Yours Felice Giardini. London, 21 July 1763.

Endeavour at Naples if you can to procure me *some boxes of flowers* of all kinds, great and small, such as are made by the Nuns, and forward them to the care of Caffarena, with Bill of Lading.

---

[36] *Fiori di penna* were flowers made from feathers and were used for embellishing stage costumes. We are grateful to Antonietta Cerocchi Pozzi for this information. The English translator obviously did not understand the significance of the phrase and left it untranslated.

No. XXIII. Giardini to Leone, 26 July 1763.

Amico Carissimo, Vengo di ricevere una lettera di Napoli d'un tal *Cosimo Maranesi*[37] il quale balla all'opera; Lui è stato quì in Londra, ma non è gran Ballerino: vorrebbe ritornare costì ma io non lo voglio; PERÒ TENETELO BELLO AFFINE VI SERVA PER BALLOTTINO. Mi scrive che ha sentito cantare due ragazze d'abilità: Io gli ho risposto che si abboccasse con voi, e lo ho ringraziato moltissimo della sua buona memoria. Questa mattina ho finito tutto l'affare con la casa, ed ho segnato; e domani comincierò ad avvertire sopra le carte pubbliche. Vi raccomando la prontezza e sollecitudine. Mi vien detto che vi sia a *Bologna* un certo *Mitchel Ballerino buono*,[38] già gli ho fatto avanzare una lettera da *Sodi*. *Credo* che Mademoiselle *Asselain*[39] voglia fare col contratto come ha fatto *Giustinelli*; gli ho dato tempo infino a domani sera; a quest'altra posta ve lo saprò dire. Intanto però se ne trovate una buona seria, tenetela a bada. Io spero che stii bene di salute e che l'affare vadi bene: non ho ricevuto altre lettere che quella di Calais.

Domani andrò in persona ad informarme della salute della vostra famiglia. Addio, mi raccomando alla vostra amicizia, e siete sicuro della mia. Tutto vostro Felice Giardini. Londra, il 26 Luglio 1763.

No. XXIV. Giardini to Leone, 5 August 1763.

Amico Carissimo, Dopo la vostra di Calais non ho più ricevuto le vostre nuove; cosa che m'inquieta un poco. La vostra moglie e figli stanno bene: Le ho dato jeri [B: gli hò dato ivi] cinque Guinee abbenchè mi disse che non le bisognava tanto, sta quasi [B: stanno quasi] sempre insieme con la moglie di Noferi. Il *Baron Bagg*[40] mi scrisse che v'aveva veduto e parlato a Parigi, e m'offerse la *Piccinelli*[41] per prima Donna. Io gli ho fatto una risposta ambigua, non sapendo nulla di quello che avete fatto finora: Spero però che riceverò per la prima posta le vostre lettere. Sto in Londra apposta, così che potrete dirigerle a me in Suffolk-street, Hay-market, London.

---

[37] Cosimo Maranesi (b. c1736) danced at the Teatro Alibert at Rome in 1765-66, where he received 200 zecchini. See Antonietta Cerocchi, 'I carnevale al Teatro Alibert o delle Dame (1766-1779)', diss. Rome (1988), p. 263. He came to London in 1752 and worked at various times at Covent Garden and the King's Theatre and also in Dublin. He performed in London from 1759 to 1763, after which nothing is known of him. See *Biographical Dictionary*, X, 87-88.

[38] Pierre Bernard Michel (fl. 1739-1790). He appeared at Covent Garden in 1740 as a child, and at Drury Lane in 1741-42 and from time to time later in the decade. He was a major performer in Lisbon, Vienna, Modena and Venice. He did not appear in London in the 1760s, but did spend time in Dublin. See *Biographical Dictionary*, X, 212-213. For Michel's agreement with Marcucci, see No. XXXVI, below.

[39] Mlle Asselain (or Asselin) danced at the King's Theatre, Haymarket, as first

No. XXIII.

Dearest Friend, I Have just received a Letter from one *Cosimo Maranesi*, who dances at the Opera: He has been in London, but he is no great Dancer. He has a mind to return here, but I will not receive him, yet keep him *at Bay* [D: in suspence], and use him as a FOOTBALL. He speaks much in favour of two young Girls, whom he has heard sing. I have directed him to address himself to you, with a thousand fine Compliments for his remembrance of me [D: thanked him mightily for his good memory]. This Day I have compleated my agreement for the Theatre [D: finished all the business about the house], and have signed it. And to-morrow I shall begin my Advertisements in the Public Papers. I recommend to you watchfulness and dispatch. I am just informed, there is one *Michell* at *Bologna*, a *good Dancer*, and have already got *Sodi* to write to him. I have reason to think *Madamoiselle Asselain* means to follow *Giustinelli*'s example. I have allowed her till to-morrow night. Next post you shall know the result. In the mean time, if you should find a good serious Dancer, keep her in suspence. I hope your health continues good, and that all our affairs go well. I have not heard from you since your Letter from Calais. To-morrow I will go to your house to enquire after your Family. Adieu, preserve me your friendship, so you are sure of mine. Felice Giardini. London, July 26, 1763.

No. XXIV.

Dearest Friend, Since your Letter from Calais, I have heard nothing from you, which makes me a little uneasy. Yesterday I gave your Wife five Guineas, (although she said she did not want so much) and found her and her children well: they are constantly with Noferi's Wife. *Baron Bagg* writes me word, he saw you, and spoke with you at Paris, and has offered me the *Piccinelli* as first Woman. I made him an ambiguous answer, not knowing what you may have done for me by this time. I am in expectation of Letters from you by the first Post. I remain in London for that purpose, so that you may direct to me in Suffolk-street, Hay-market, London. I conclude not knowing what

---

woman from 1760 to 1763 and rejoined the company for 1765-66. She was apparently Polly Capitani's teacher (see note 43, below). See *Biographical Dictionary*, I, 142.

[40] Charles Ernest, Baron de Bagge (1722-1791), whose musical salon in Paris was famous. See G. Cucuel, 'Le Baron de Bagge et son temps', *L'année musicale*, no. 1 (1912), 145-186; *New Grove*, II, 16-17; and Appendix A, No. XXXVII, below. Baron Bagge was a wealthy and eccentric instrument collector who had studied the violin with Tartini. He appears as a character in E. T. A. Hoffman's 'Die Serapionsbrüder' (1819) and as Crespin in Act III of Offenbach's *Les contes d'Hoffman*.

[41] Probably Anna Maria Piccinelli, who sang roles in operas by Guglielmi and Bertoni in Venice at the Teatro S. Benedetto in 1767.

Finirò per non saper più cosa dire, non potendo fissare nulla senza prima ricevere le vostre lettere. Addio; credetemi di tutto cuore. Vostro amico e servo Felice Giardini.

Noferi e Mr. Farmer vi salutano.

No. XXV. Giardini to Leone, 12 August 1763.

Caro Leone, *Mi spiace all'anima di sentire il disappuntamento che avete trovata in Parigi*. Ciò è colpa mia non avendo *prima inviato* una lettera d'avviso all[a] Vedova (*) *Magra*, come pure quello di Caffarena toccante il Signor Marchesio. Subito ricevuto la vostra, sono andato a dare gli ordini opportuni a Caffarena ed al ricever di queste, riceverete a Roma come pure a Napoli tutte quelle sicurtà e denaro necessario. Intanto fate presto, e scrivetemi subito che n'avrete impegnato qualcheduno. Oggi scriverò a *Graziani*[42] gli dirò che a riguardo vostro surmonterò le difficoltà che vi sono A METTER FUORI IL VIOLONCELLO DELLA R...... NON OSTANTE SARÀ FUORI; io non so che scrivervi, atteso che più istruzioni di quelle che v'ho dato sarebbero di nissun uso; e così non posso dirvi altro se non che la vostra moglie sta bene, le ho dato cinque guinee, il figliuolo sta bene come pure la ragazza: Fatene altrettanto e credetemi di tutto cuore vostro amico e servo Felice Giardini.

Caffarena, Noferi, Giustinelli, Farmer, Polly[43] vi salutano caramente. Noferi è in campagna.

(*) Plaisanterie à la Giardini pour dire la Veuve Grasse [this footnote not in B].

No. XXVa. Gennaro Magri in Vienna to Leone, 18 August 1763.[44]

Carissimo Amico Scusi se non risposi a posta corrente alla sua carissima Lettera ma mi fu data doppo qualche Tempo che era in posta ne provai un dispiacere grandissimo pazienza in somma sento con piacere le vostre fortune Io caro amico molto volontière accetterei la vostra proposta ma io sono ingagiato per tutto questo Anno e sono ben paghato e posso stare quanti anni che voglio in soma io vi parlerò d'amico io qui hò sei cento Zecchini e viaggi paghati onde veda io voglio mostrare della Amicizia ma vorei anco non sacrificarmi in tutto si che volendo che io venchi io voglio sette Cento Zecchini e un beneficio per me e credo esser discreto al mio grado e poi si dice per proverbio che chi più spende meno spende onde in tal Caso io chiederò la licenza a benchè la veda deficilissima ma se non l'averò per farvi piacere la prenderò per forza si che da lei dipende il tutto io sto attendendo la risposta di qualunque maniere e gli sia per mia regola non mi manchi e sono

---

[42] Cellist in Paris; see No. XXXVII, below.
[43] Probably Polly Capitani, daughter of the opera tailor, a child dancer who made her King's Theatre début in 1759 at the age of seven. See *Biographical Dictionary*, III, 44.

Appendix A

more to say, as I cannot fix any thing till I hear from you. Adieu. Believe me cordially   Your friend and servant Felice Giardini.
   Noferi and Mr. Farmer send their compliments.

No. XXV.
Dear Leone, Your disappointment at Paris has hurt me to the quick. It is my *fault*, by not having sent a Letter of advice to the Widow *Lean* (*) [D: Widow *Magro* (a nick name)]. I am equally vexed at Caffarena's disappointing you in credit on Mr. Marchesio. On the receipt of yours, I went to direct him to give the necessary orders, so that on the receipt of this you will have all the credit and security you can require both at Rome and Naples. In the mean while make haste, and the instant you have contracted with any one, let me know it. I will write by this Day's Post to Graziani, to let him know. I will on your recommendation wave all difficulties IN STRIKING OUT THE VIOLINCELLO OF THE Q. . . . . [D: violencello of the K.] WHO SHALL CERTAINLY BE OUT. I know not what to write. Any instructions beyond those I have given you would be useless, and therefore I have nothing to say, but that your Family is all well. I have given your Wife five Guineas. [D adds:] Your son is well as is the Girl. Believe me cordially Yours Felice Giardini.
   Caffarena, Noferi, Giustinelli, Farmer, Polly send their compliments. Noferi is in the Country.
   (*) An attempt to wit; meaning the Widow *Grasse*. Grasse in French signifying *Fat*.

No. XXVa.
Dearest Friend Excuse my not answering your Letter by the return of the post but it was given me some time after it had layn in the Post Office which gave me great uneasiness but Patience in fine I hear of your good fortune with pleasure I would dear ffriend accept your proposal willingly But I am Engaged for the whole year and am well paid and can be here as many Years as I please in fine I will speak to you as a friend I have here six hundred sequins and my Journeys paid whence see I will shew my ffriendship for you but I must not sacrifice myself altogether so that if you chuse I should come I will have 700 Sequins and a benefit to myself and I believe my self discreet in my rank besides the proverb says—he that spends most spends least, wherefore in such a Case I would apply for Leave although I know it would be difficult but If I cannot get it to do you pleasure I will take it by force so that on this depends the whole I wait your Answer whatever it may be for my rule to go by.

---

44   Source: C12/517/16. The scribe spells the name 'Mogri'. We have not attempted to correct the grammar of this letter, which is only semi-literate. The lack of punctuation, which makes this letter so difficult to decipher, is typical of Magri's writing style, as can be seen in his *Trattato teorico-prattico di ballo* (Naples, 1779).

P.S. Per la compagnia che ho al presente non vol [voi] far tali passi al presente non sapendo chi siano l'impresarii e non conoscendovi e poi perche il suo tempo non e finito ma vi dirò che potrà scrivere alla Madelena formigli Mora[45] che è a Venezia o pure alla [blank] che ancora [blank] che sta fermata per il Carnevale a Milano puol darsi che venchi e faccia come fo io se ci agiustiamo in fine mi diar e si fidi che farò quel che posso e vi farò onore sicuro addio vero vostro Genero Magri.

No. XXVI. Giardini to Leone at Naples, 22 August 1763.

Amico caro, Veramente dovrei farvi un *mondo di Apologie per quello* che mi dite *essere stato disappuntato*; Ma se l'avessi saputo da Parigi, allora il rimedio sarebbe stato più pronto; nulla di meno non serve perdersi di coraggio, perchè il danaro si troverà, e come vi scrissi nella mia antecedente, l'ordine è mandato tanto per Roma come pure per Napoli. Non mi manca altro che quello che appartiene a voi: non fate il difficile, se veramente questo Mazziotti è *così bravo*. Se la *Brucciatina* si mette a cosa onesta va bene, se no mi è stato rotto il capo dal *Baron Bagg* per questa *Piccinelli*. Mi stupisco di sentire che in Italia non si possa ritrovar soggetti come la *Sartori* e *Giustinelli* per quel prezzo: Bisogna dunque credere, che tutta la *Musica* è partita d'Italia ed è andata a far *villeggiatura* in *Germania* ed in *Olanda*: Non importa. Venghiamo a questi due ballerini abbenchè raggazzi se l'offerta di 600 Zechini ò 700 e pagargli i viaggi a venire qui, gli accomoda, potrete fermargli. Non mancate d'impegnare questo (†) *Pasticciere* e se *Piccini* non puol rompere il suo ingaggiamento, fate in sorte d'avere la sua musica; e se *ne vuole comporre una apposta per me* gli lascio l'arbitrio del Drama, e gli farò un regalo *di 80 Zecchini*: e questo gli potrà fare un nome, ed un'intratura in questo paese, che gli recherà gran avantaggio per quando sarà per portarsi lui stesso. *Romani viene*. Ricordatevi di queste *due ragazze*. Scrivetemi un poco più sovente, affinchè se mancasse qualche cosa vi si possa rimediare a tempo. La lettera del *Todi* è veramente pellegrina; non credo che vi sia grande necessità a rimandarla, ma pure la terrò ben custodita, ed in caso che potesse portare qual che pregiudizio, ve la rimanderò subitamente: già l'ho fatta registrare al libro. La vostra moglie e famiglia stanno tutti bene, tutti i miei amici vi salutano. *Cattolino* sta con l'aspettativa di poter urinare. I *Deamicis*[46] sono disperatissimi in

---

[45] Maddalena Formigli, known as 'La Mora', danced at Venice between 1753 and 1765.
[46] A famous family of singers and dancers. Giardini is probably referring to Anna Lucia and her [father?] Domenico De Amicis. The patriarch was Domenico Antonio (b. Fermo, c1716), a *tenore buffo*; his wife, Rosalba Baldacci (b. Atri, Teramo, c1716), was a soprano. Anna Lucia De Amicis Buonsollazzi was the best known member of the family. She made her début at Bologna in 1755 before embarking on a highly successful career which took her to Paris, Brussels, Vienna, Milan, Venice, Naples and London.

P.S. as to the Partner I have at present she will not take such steps at present not knowing who the Managers are or being Acquainted with them and because her Term is not yet finished but I will tell you you may write to the Madelena Formigli Mora who is at Venice or to the [blank] Allso there and who is Engaged for the Carnival at Milan it may be she will Come and do as I do If we can Agree in the mean time I shall do as much as I can and shall certainly do you Honor Adieu Genaro Mogri.

No. XXVI.

Dearest Friend, In truth I should make you *many Apologies* for the *Disappointment* you met with at Paris. Had I known it sooner, the remedy should have been quicker; nevertheless, do not be dismayed, because money will be found, and as I wrote you word in my last, the order is sent as well to Rome as Naples. I want nothing but what depends on you. *Do not make difficulties if this Mazziotti is so good.* If the *Brucciatina* will come on reasonable terms, it is well; if not, I am tormented by *Baron Bagg* in favour of *Piccinelli*. I am much surprized, that *such Subjects*, as the *Sartori* and *Giustinelli*, are *not* to be *found* in *Italy*, and for the same price. I am to conclude then, that *all Music has deserted Italy* to turn *Stroller* in *Holland* and *Germany*. No matter; let us come to these two Dancers. Young as they are, if they will take 6 or 700 Sequins, and their Journey to England free, you may engage them. Do not fail engaging this (†) *Pasticiere*, and if *Piccini* cannot break off his engagement, endeavour to get his Music. If he will compose an Opera on purpose for me, I will leave him the choice of the Subject [D: I leave the Drama to him], and give him 80 *Sequins* for it. This may gain him credit and acquaintance in this Country, which may prove very beneficial to him against he comes over himself. *Romani comes*. Remember the *two* young Girls. Write to me oftener, that if any thing be wanting, it may be remedied in time. Todi's Letter is really strange. I see no great occasion to send it back. But I will keep it safe, and in case it should be of any prejudice to him, will return it forthwith. I have already had it entered in my Book. Your Wife and Family are well. My Friends send their compliments. [D adds: Catolini is in hopes of being able to piss.] The *De Amicis* are in Holland in despair, not knowing where to go. *Giustinelli* is in the

---

She performed *buffa* roles with considerable success at the King's Theatre, Haymarket, in 1762-63, and was given parts in the serious operas *Orione* and *Zanaida* by J. C. Bach. She went on to become a long-time performer of serious opera in Naples; Mozart heard her there in Jommelli's *Armida abbandonata* and created for her the part of Giunia in *Lucio Silla*. In 1778 she sang in the first Italian performance of Gluck's *Alceste*; she retired from the stage in 1788. See *DEUMM*, Le Biografie, II, 420, and *Biographical Dictionary*, IV, 245-247.

Olanda per non saper dove andare. *Giustinelli* è andato alla campagna ed io sto quì a travagliare per metter in ordine la casa dell'Opera: Addio. Ricordatevi dei comandamenti abbenchè ve ne faccio Plenipotenziario con una certa tal quale moderazione. Sempre di tutto cuore. Vostro Felice Giardini. Londra al di 22 Agusto 1763.
(†) Mr. Vento.

No. XXVII. Giardini to Leone at Rome [undated; before 22 August 1763?].

Amico carissimo, *Quanto la vostra ultima me abbia fatto dispiacere*, ve lo lascio immaginare; ma la colpa non è mia: con tutto ciò troverete tutto rimediato; ROMANI VERRÀ, COSICHE NON MI BISOGNA ALTRO CHE IL PRIM' UOMO E LA PRIMA DONNA, la *Spagnioletta* se si puole ed il *Basso* e le due ragazze: una coppia da ballerini, se *non si ritrova la coppia*, mi BASTERÀ UNA BRAVA GROTTESCA. Tengo tre ballerini eccellenti: sappiate che la seconda e terza donna la ho ed il second'uomo: non v'imbarazzate per l'altr'anno che ho già trovato tesori, travagliate a questo anno, e NON BADATE A' MIEI PREZZI; giachè siamo così tardi, so che in queste occasioni, vorranno tirarmi per la gola, ma pazienza. Giacchè ho fissato tutto quì, bisogna cercar nient'altro che una *decente economia*, ed addatata alle presenti circostanze. Subito mando dalla vostra moglie le vostre nuove ed il danaro, lei e la famiglia stanno benissimo: Contate sopra me che prenderò Graziani, anzi gli farò parlare da Venier.[47] Quì si dice che il matrimonio della sorella del Re si farà nel mese di Novembre; Dunque, se potessi cominciare le mie prove nel mese d'Ottobre, sarebbe una buona cosa. Scrivimi sempre, quando non fosse che quattro righe, e diriggi le mie lettere così: To Mr. Giardini in great Suffolk-street Hay-Market, London. Toccante a Piccini, sicuramente avrei piacere d'averlo, ma quando non si possa, bisognerà aver dell'opere intiere delle meglio; ed allora prendere quello che voi m'avete detto. Oggi ho fatto spedire altre lettere per Roma e Napoli, cosicchè vi diriggo questa a Napoli. Addio state sano, di tutto cuore mi dico vostro amico e servo Felice Giardini. Londra.

No. XXVIIa. Giardini to Leone [undated].[48]

Amico Caro, Doppo spedito l'altre Lettere mi viene una Lettera della Cità della quale bisogna che v'avisi di Passare da i Signori Wills e Leigh gli quali vi soministerranno dennari e sicurta: addio caro Leone la posta parte sempre vostro F Giardini.

---

[47] Probably Jean Baptiste Venier (fl. 1755-1784), music publisher in Paris. See *New Grove*, XIX, 621.

Appendix A

Country, and I remain here labouring to get the Theatre in order. Adieu. Remember the Commandments, as I make you my *Plenipotentiary*, tho' with a certain reserve. I am ever cordially Yours Felice Giardini. London, *Aug.* 22, 1763.

(†) Mr. Vento.

No. XXVII.

Dearest Friend, *I Leave you to imagine how much your last has vexed me*, although it is not my fault. With all this you will find every thing remedied. ROMANI COMES, SO THAT I WANT ONLY A FIRST MAN, A FIRST WOMAN SINGER, (the *Spagnioletta* if possible) and a Bass, the two Girls, a couple of Dancers, or in default of them, ONE GOOD WOMAN COMIC DANCER, as I have already *three excellent Men Dancers*. I have also the *second* and *third Women Singers*, and the *second Man*. I am already provided for next year, therefore confine your attention to this Year, and

PAY NO REGARD TO MY PRICES.

The Season is far advanced, and I am aware that on such occasions, they will make the most of me [D: they will draw me by the throat]; but patience. As I have fixed every thing here, you have only to mind a *decent Oeconomy*, adapted to the present circumstances. Your Wife and Family are well. I shall immediately supply her with money, and send her news of you. Be assured I will take Graziani, and will get Venier to speak to him. It is reported, the King's Sister is to be married in November. If then I could begin my Rehearsals in October, I should find my account in it. Continue writing to me, although it should be but four lines, and direct to Mr. Felice Giardini, in great Suffolk-street, Hay-market, London. With regard to Piccini, certainly I should like to have him; but if that cannot be, it will be necessary to get some of the best entire Operas, and in that case to take the Person (*) you mentioned to me. I send other Letters by this Day's Post to Rome and Naples; so that I direct this to Naples. Adieu. Keep well. I am cordially your friend and Servant, Felice Giardini.

(*) Mr. Vento.

No. XXVIIa.

Dear ffriend Since I dispatched the other Letter I have a Letter from the City by which it is necessary you should have Notice to go to Messrs. Wills and Leigh who will give you money and security Adieu Dear Leone the Post is going out allways yours F. Giardini.

---

[48] Source: C12/517/16.

No. XXVIIb. Clementina Spagnioli in Venice to Leone, 27 August 1763.[49]

Monsieur, Accuso d'aver receuta la sua favoritissima in data de tredici corrente unitamente all' invito per il Real Teatro di Londra sopra di ciò significo a V.S. essendo io avanzata in altro trattato onde la brevità e la stretessa del Tempo converebbe che io dimetessi al' sopra detta stretto trattato e non potendosi trà noi convenire in una semplice lettera bramarò in altra occasione dimostrarle il desiderio di poterla servire come aurei [avrei] procurato se si fosse discorso à voce in tanto la ringrazio della sua attenzione che hà avuto di favorirmi e mi dichiaro sua serva umilissima devotissima ed obbligatissima serva Clementina Spagnioli.

No. XXVIII. Giardini to Leone, 30 August 1763.

Carissimo amico, Ricevo la vostra del 10 corrente la quale non mi fa poco dispiacere in sentire quanto siano grandi le calamità; ma spero che a quest'ora saranno finite e che avrete ritrovato tutto. ORA SENTITE BENE, A ME NON MI BISOGNA ALTRO CHE IL SOPRANO PRIM'UOMO ED IL BASSO e gli due ballerini che mi dite d'aver impegnato; Se non avete fissato con la *Spagnioletta*, come mi pare, non impegnate nissuna, perchè avrò la *Mingotti*. Eccoci adunque in porto; tutto quello che mi preme è che vi ritroviate quì al più lungo tempo alla fine del mese venturo ò per la metà d'Ottobre con il *prim'uomo* ed il *Basso* ed i Ballerini, e quelle *due ragazze*, se le trovate.

IN QUANTO ALLA CASSA NON HO AVUTO TEMPO D'INFORMARMI, MA CREDO CHE SARÀ DIFFICILE FARLA ENTRARE SENZA DOGANA, PARTICOLARMENTE VENENDO PER MARE, FUORCHÈ IL CAPITANO DEL VASCELLO FOSSE VOSTRO INTIMO AMICO, ED ALLORA POI TROVERESSIMO MODO DI AVER LA ROBBA APPOCO APPOCO IN UNA MANIERA COMODA E SENZA RISCHIO.

Se non potete aver Piccini, scritturate subito questo Signor Vento tanto per comporre un'Opera come pure per accomodar le altre e recite, e tutte quelle addizioni che occorrerano nella stagione e fatelo partire con gli altri. Se potete fare che si ritroviano tutti quì alla fine del mese prossimo potrei andar in scena verso la fine d'Ottobre, che sarà il tempo del matrimonio della Principessa.

La vostra moglie sta bene e tutta la famiglia ancora. Addio, caro amico fate il più presto possibile che mi sarà d'un grandissimo vantaggio: UN ALTR'ANNO GIÀ FAREMO MEGLIO atteso che quasi tengo la compagnia tutta fatta. Salutatemi tutti gli amici e credetemi con tutta l'amicizia vostro amico e servo Felice Giardini. Londra.

Nel progetto del Ballo, gli leverò solamente quella figura dell' IMPRESARIO INTENERITO.

---

[49] Source: C12/517/16.

Appendix A

No. XXVIIb.
Sir I acknowledge the favor of yours of the 13th instant containing an Invitation for the Royal Theatre in London upon this I signify to you that being Advanced in another Treaty and the shortness of the time requiring that I should give up the aforesaid strict Contract and I not being able in a simple Letter to agree together I shall wish on another Occasion to shew you the desire of being able to serve you as I would have done could we have talked Vivo Voice [sic] in the mean time I thank you for your Attention to favor me and declare my self yours &c Clementina Spagnioli.

No. XXVIII.
Dearest Friend, The Account you give me in your Letter of the 10th instant of the greatness of your Distress vexes me extremely. I hope by this time there is an end of it, and that all is set to right: Now THEN UNDERSTAND ME WELL, I WANT ONLY A FIRST MAN AND A BASS, *and the two Dancers you tell me you have engaged. If you have not fixed with the Spagnioletta*, (as it seems) *do not engage any one as I shall have the Mingotti*. Here we are then safe in Port. All my concern now is, that you should be here at farthest by the end of next Month, or the middle of October, with the *first Man*, the *Bass*, the *Dancers*, and these *two Girls, if you can get them.*

    WITH REGARD TO THE BOX, I HAVE NOT HAD TIME TO INFORM MYSELF, BUT BELIEVE, IT WILL BE DIFFICULT TO GET IT WITHOUT PAYING THE DUTY, ESPECIALLY AS IT COMES BY SEA, UNLESS THE CAPTAIN OF THE SHIP HAPPENS TO BE YOUR INTIMATE FRIEND, IN WHICH CASE WE CAN CONTRIVE TO HAVE THE MERCHANDISE BY LITTLE AND LITTLE WITHOUT ANY RISQUE.

    If you cannot get Piccini, *contract immediately with Mr. Vento*, to compose one Opera, as well as to patch up others [D: to put others together], and make Recitative, and such other Additions as may be requisite in the course of the Season, and send him away with the rest. If you can contrive to send them all over by the end of next Month, I might begin my Operas by the end of October, which will be the time of the Princess's Marriage. Your Family is all well. Adieu, dear Friend, make all the haste you can for my advantage. ANOTHER YEAR WE WILL DO BETTER, as I have almost fixed the whole Company. My compliments to all Friends, and believe me with the greatest friendship your Friend and servant Felice Giardini.

    In the Project of the Dance I will only leave out the Character of the MANAGER HUMANIZED.

No. XXIX. A. D. Varese at Genoa to Leone at Naples, 3 September 1763.

Dagli Signori *Moris* e *Caffarena* di Londra mi è stato ordinato di fornirle costì una lettera di credito per potersene valere alle sue occorrenze per la somma di lire duecento sterline; pertanto le compiego l'inclusa lettera diretta a cotesti Signori *Jermey* [sic] & *Merry* Negozianti, i quali hanno ordine dal Signore *Giuseppe Brame* di fornirlo di parte o tutta detta somma ad ogni sua richiesta, ed in caso di qualche esigenza gliene passerà la dovuta ricevuta. Questa sera le scrivo parimenti altra mia lettera a V: S: diretta per *Roma* con un altro credito di simil somma che le serva d'avviso. Li sudditti Signori *Moris* e *Caffarena* m'avvisano parimenti d'ordinare a qualche negoziante di costì di garantire a quelli virtuosi che accorderà, le scritture che le farà in caso che avessero qualche dubbio: ma questo, per mancanza d'amico costì di confidenza, non ho potuto effettuare, ma in caso di bisogno, potrà offrire la mia garanzia qui che sarò pronto a darla e con facilità si potrà combinare per mezzo di negozianti di costì: Si compiacia avvisarmi l'occorrenze per mia regola, e col desiderio di servirla mi protesto. Devotissimo Obbligatissimo Servo Agostino Domenico Varese.

No. XXX. Giardini to Leone, 8 September 1763.

Amico Carissimo, Ricevo la vostra del 19. passato da Firenze. Mi dispiace all'anima, che non vi siete portato a *Roma* ò a *Napoli* subito atteso che così erano le istruzioni ed io non vi ho scritto che a *Roma* ed a *Napoli*; cosicchè vi prego caldamente a lasciar andare tutte quelle Romane per belle che sieno, giacchè sono impegnate, nè di pensare all'anno prossimo, che è quest'anno che mi preme. ADESSO VI REPLICO CHE NON HO BISOGNO CHE DEL PRIM'UOMO ED IL BASSO con quella coppia di Ballerini che dite d'aver impegnati: questo mi farà, essendo provvisto di tutto il resto. Se trovate quelle RAGAZZE DI BUONA VOCE E BELLE, conducetele. Fate tutti i vostri sforzi di ritrovarvi [B: ritrovarsi] in Londra nella prima settimana d'Ottobre, senza questo sono rovinato. A Napoli, come vi scrissi nella mia ultima troverete quel danaro che v'occorre. Addio, se mi siete veramente amico come lo spero, lasciamo andare le barzellette, e venite qui con gli altri il più presto possibile. Vi mando una copia di questa anche a *Napoli*. La vostra moglia sta bene e le ho dato dell'altro dennaro; cosichè non le manca null'altra cosa che la vostra compagnia. Mi dico di tutto cuore Vostro sincero Amico Felice Giardini.

No. XXIX.
I am directed by Mess. *Morris* and *Caffarena* of London to furnish you with Credit for 200 £. on Naples, and for this purpose send you the Letter inclosed for Mess. *Jerney* [sic] and *Merry*, Merchants there, who have orders from Mr. *Giuseppe Brame* to honour your draughts for the said Sum or any part of it, which you may require: in which case you will give the usual receipt. I write to you also by this Post directed at *Rome*, with the like Credit; which may serve you as a Letter of advice. Mess. *Morris* and *Caffarena* also direct me to procure some Merchant there, to become security to such persons [D: such Virtuosi] as you shall contract with, in case they should require it. This I could not comply with for want of a friend there; but in case of necessity, you may offer my security here, which I shall be ready to give you, if you can get any Merchants there to go halves with me. Please to advise me of the receipt of this, and believe me &c. Agostino Dom. Varese.

No. XXX.
Dearest Friend, I Have received yours of the 19th of last Month from Florence, and am much displeased that you did not repair to Rome or Naples immediately, according to your instructions, as I have directed to you no where else. I entreat you to leave all the Roman Women, though never so handsome, as they are all engaged, and not to think about next year, but about this only. *I again repeat to you*, I WANT ONLY A FIRST MAN, A BASS, and the *couple of Dancers*, which you tell me you have engaged, having provided all the rest myself. If you can get two HANDSOME YOUNG GIRLS with good voices, bring them with you. Get to London if possible by the first week in October, or I shall be ruined. You will find what money you want at Naples, as I told you in my last. Adieu. If you have any value for me, let us leave off joking, and repair to London with the rest as fast as possible. I send a Copy of this to *Naples*. Your Wife is well, and I have given her more money, so that she wants for nothing but your company. I am cordially Your sincere friend Felice Giardini.

No. XXXI. Giardini to Leone, 16 September 1763.

Amico Carissimo, V'Aspetto con grandissima ansietà: NON MI MANCATE TOCCANTE IL BASSO, che è UNA COSA CHE MI PREME MOLTISSIMO. Ora vi diro una più bella: La *Cremonini* non sarà più all'Opera atteso che il suo padre non ha segnato il contratto, *cosichè mi preme d'avere un'ultima parte*. Se queste *due ragazze* non si trovano, trovate almeno una buona figura di donna, che come vi puotete imaginare dovrà fare da uomo, oppure un qualche castrato giovine ma con buona voce, e per questa ultima parte, non vi estendete più di 400 zecchini. Sono adesso quatro settimane che non ricevo le vostre nuove. Tutto il resto concernente all'Opera è già in ordine, cosichè ricordatevi che il tempo passa: Dal momento che le vostre lettere m'annoncieranno il vostro arrivo a Torino, vi farò toccare del dennaro a vista da un Banchiere che non sarà così *Viso di Cazzo* come il Signor Marchesio. Quella casa Willis a Napoli, mi vien detto che farà onore a tutto quello che vi bisogna; in tal caso potete fare delle tratte sopra di me, ma badate che siano fatte da pagarsi nel mese di Gennaro prossimo.

Dopo questa non vi scrivero più a Napoli, perchè spero che partirete subito, senza questo sarei rovinato per sempre: Così vi replico amico caro non perdete tempo a strologare per l'anno prossimo; partite con la compagnia subito e fate in sorte d'essere qui almeno la prima o seconda settimana del mese intrante. Addio con tutto il cuore. Vostro Amico e servo Felice Giardini. Londra.

P.S. Per l'ordinario prossimo potrete in caso di bisogno, se l'altro vi manca, indirizzarvi al Signor Marchese *Quarantotto*, al quale per sicuro gli saranno dati gli ordini opportuni al mio nome.

No. XXXII. Pietro Giovanetti for Giardini to Leone, 23 September 1763.[50]

Caro Leone, Mi vien assicurato che il Re di Prussia farà l'Opera; ora dunque non *potrò aver Romani* il *Tenore*, così che fate in sorte, d'aver uno. Se non puotete trovar meglio, prendete il *Cattaneo*. La posta parte, così non vi posso dir altro, non mancate in questo. La copia di questa vi sarà rimessa a Turino, ed a Milano, Tutto vostro Pietro Giovanetti, *per* Felice Giardini. Londra.

Nel vostro corso informatevi e trattate con qualche bravo *Pittore di Sciene*.

---

[50] Giovanetti was Giardini's assistant manager for 1763-64.

Appendix A

No. XXXI.

Dearest Friend, I am expecting you with the greatest impatience. DO NOT FAIL PROCURING ME A BASS, AS IT IS OF THE UTMOST CONSEQUENCE TO ME. Here is news for you [D: I will tell you a cleaverer thing]: The *Cremonini* is not to belong to the Opera, her Father not having signed the Contract; *so that I now want a Singer for the last part*. Therefore if you cannot get the *two Girls*, endeavour to engage a Woman of a good figure, who, as you may imagine, must occasionally perform in Mens Cloaths, or a young Castrato with a good voice; but do not exceed 400 Sequins. It is now four weeks since I have heard from you. All else relating to the Opera, is now in course. Remember, time passes. The moment I have advice of your arrival at Turin, I will send you Credit on a Banker less (*) *scrupulous* than Mr. *Marchesio*. I am told the House of *Wills* and *Leigh* at Naples will honour your draughts for what money you may want, so that you may draw Bills on me; but beware of making them payable before next January. After this I shall no longer direct to you at Naples, as I hope you will leave it immediately, without which I shall be ruined for ever. Dear Friend, let me remind you not to lose time in providing for next year. Set out with the Company immediately, and get here by the first or second week of next Month, at farthest. Adieu. I am cordially Yours &c. Felice Giardini.

P.S. By next post you may in case of need, if the other fails you, apply to the Marquis *Quarantotto*, who shall have proper directions from me.

(*) The Original is so vulgar and indecent, that it will not bear Translation.[51]

No. XXXII.

Dear Leone, I Am just assured the King of Prussia intends to have an Opera, and that *I cannot have Romani*. Therefore endeavour to have a *Tenor*, and take *Cattaneo* if you cannot get a better. The Post is going out, so that I can say no more. Do not fail in this. You will receive a Copy of this Letter at Turin and Milan.—Wholly Yours Pietro Giovanetti, *for* Felice Giardini. London, Sept. 23, 1763.

In your Journey enquire after, and treat with some *good Scene-Painter*.

---

[51] 'Viso di cazzo': literally, 'prick face'.

No. XXXIIa. Receipt from Antonio Baini in Rome to Leone, 4 October 1763.[52]

Io sottoscritto hò ricevuto dal Signor Gabriele Leone incaricato di procura dal Signor Felice Giardini come Impressario del Teatro di Londra Zecchini cento cinquanta effettivi quali sono a conto dell' Zecchini cinque cento che vengono accordati secondo l'apoca fra di noi stata sottoscritta per la recita della Signora Cecilia Baini mia Consorte alla quale in tutto e per tutto da ambe le parti si abbia ragione obbligandomi io sottoscritto di essere in Lione di Francia con la sudetta Signora Cecilia Baini mia Consorte nel corso di Giorni venti principiando tal termine dal dì sei del corrente mese di ottobre senza potere addurre alcuna scusa ò pretesto salva però la malatia (che Iddio non voglia) che potesse accedere alta [alla] detta mia Consorte obbligandomi e dato a mio nome proprio che di mia consorte sudetta nella più ampla forma della Reverenda Camera Apostolica con le solite Clausole In fede Roma questo dì et anno sudetto 4 Ottobre 1763. Io Antonio Baini mi obligo come sopra Cecilia Baini.

No. XXXIIb. F. Barazzi in Rome to Leone, 'li 7 [gennaio?] del 1764'.[53]

Riceuta che ebbi la sua Lettera da Milano non mancai di fare le doute diligenze per vedere se fosse stato quì portato il pachetto indicatomi in essa ma non fu possibile di rinuenirle ne scrissi subbito in Milano al Signor Combe come mi diceste che dovevo fare sapere la riceuta da esso mai o avuta sua risposta ne piu ò pensato a questo affare ora che mi fa la nova istanza sarò un giorno per sapere quando il Corriere Gio: Testone sarrà qui di ritorno in Roma e le ne farò istanza et allora lo farò avere alli Signori Willes et Leigh di Napoli io però le scrissi costà che doveva sapere che questa Robba deve pagare vendario in Napoli che però era necessario che lei lo sapesse onde novamente la torno a fare questa nota per evitare quelli inconvenienti che potessero accaderle mi spiace che l'amico di Genova mancasse di farle pagare in Lione il danaro come a me fece sapere che avrebbe fatto positivamente di tutto ne fui inteso dal Sr. Mayeure di Lione al quale mi lusingo che averà r'imborsata la somma che avanzò secondo à me scrisse onde questa notizia mi sarà grata saperla avero un vero piacere di udire delle buone nove dell'incontro del Signor Vento e Signora Baini che ad ambi le prego di riverire in mio nome è divotissimo. . . . Francesco Barazzi.

---

[52] Source: C12/517/16.
[53] Source: C12/517/16.

Appendix A

No. XXXIIa.

I underwritten have received from Mr. Gabriel Leone Attorney of Mr. Felice Giardini as Manager of the Theatre in London Sequins One hundred and fifty Effective which are on account of sequins five hundred that have been agreed to according to the Contract by us subscribed for the salary of Mrs. Cecilia Baini my Wife to which in all and for all both parties shall have their Right and I the under written Oblige myself to be in Lyons in ffrance with the said Cecilia my Wife within the space of Twenty days to begin from the Sixth Instant month of October without being allowed to produce any Excuse or pretext save sickness which God forbid that may happen to my said Wife Obliging myself in my own name as well as that of my said Wife abovesaid in the Amplest fform of the reverend Apostilic Chamber with the usual Clauses &c In Witness Roma the day and year abovesaid 4th October 1763 I Antonio Baini Oblige my self as above. Cecilia Baini.

No. XXXIIb.

As soon as I received your Letter from Milan I did not fail the Greatest Diligence to find out if the Packet you mentioned was brought here but it was not Possible to find it out I wrote Immediately to Mr. Combe at Milan as you told me to let him know it if I received it to which I never had an answer [nor][54] have I thought more of this Business as you now Apply to me again I shall watch to know when the courier Geo. Sestone Returns to Rome and I will ask him about it and then I will deliver it to Messrs. Wills and Leigh at Naples Besides I have written to you that this Packet must pay a Duty in Naples which was necessary that yours should [MS damaged] wherefore I repeat it to you again to avoid any inconvenience which might arise. It displeases me that the ffriend at Genoa neglected to give you Credit at Lyons for the money which he told me he would positively do: all this I Learnt from Mr. Mayevori [sic] from Lyons and to which I believe you would have reimbursed him the sum he Advanced According as he has Wrote to me wherefore I should be glad to know it[.] I should be much pleased to hear that Mr. Vento and Mrs. Baini had met with Success to whom I beg my Compliments and disposed to serve you I remain with true Esteem &c Francesco B[a]razzi.

---

[54] MS damaged and not legible.

No. XXXIII. Berardi's affidavit, 4 July 1764.[55]

Dichiarazione di Luigo [sic] Berardi li 4 Luglii 1764. Avendo aspettato a Parigi circa un mese di tempo sull'aspettativa di recevere danaro dal *Giardini* per proseguir il viaggio e non avendo mai ricevuta alcuna rimessa, mi portai in Londra mediante l'ajuto della Signora *Tognoni*[56] quì chiamata da *Giardini* per cantare, e subito giunto a Londra verso alla fine di Gennajo scorso, fui invitato dal detto *Giardini* per mezzo del Signor *Sodi* alle prove per cominciar le mie fatiche; ciò non ostante non mi fu mai possibile di ricevere alcun danaro dal detto *Giardini*, prolungandomi il pagamento secondo il mio contratto fatto con il Signor *Leone* suo agente. Perlocchè dicendomi che questo contratto non era valido, mi forzò, conoscendomi miserabile, e molto bisognoso di danaro ed abito per comparire, di far nuovo contratto col ribassamento di 45 Lire Sterline in circa dalla prima paga, che era di 200. Zecchini; e perciò fui necessitato di contentarmi a tanto per settimana, pro rata della quale somma dovutami, mi resta debitore di 20 Lire Sterline in circa, non ostante che il contratto espressamente dica di pagarmi ogni settimana pro rata, e di essermi adoperato più volte per ricevere questa somma.

Io dichiaro che questa è la pura verità.

Londra   Luigi Berardi

No. XXXIV. Ravaschiello in Paris to Leone in London, 30 April 1764.[57]

Stimatissimo Signore, Sono già passati cinque mesi, che per mia disgrazia mi ritrovo quì a Parigi sulle spese: e senza annojarvi di dirvi tutte le cose minuto per minuto, basta dirvi che ho fatto il conto a secco a secco, e fra tutto il mio dispendio, fra la camera fra il mangiare ed il bere mattina e sera fra le candele ed il fuoco che mi alluminavano nella camera quando sono stato malato, e fra tutto viene ad essere il conto a tre lire il giorno che io devo pagare. Come ben sa il Signor *Gabriele Leone* che io sono restato senza nessuna sorte di moneta quando sono venuto quì a Parigi: Che quello poco che avevo, vedendo che lui in Lione non aveva più denari io glieli diedi; Onde io devo pagare qui in Parigi 5 mesi a ragione di 3 Lire il giorno; dove ho lasciato la mia valigia con tutta la musica che io avevo con ancora gli stivali, la mia mostra, le fibbie di brillo che io avevo, tutti stanno in mano di questi Signori. Onde io non domando altro: nè vi metto avanti agl'occhi tutto quelle che avrei guadagnato in tutto questo tempo che sono stato quì non solo senza far niente; ma è stata tanta la collera che ho avuta, che mi ha fatto cascar malato; e credevo che per ricompensa di tutto, perdevo ancora la vita: Onde non vi domando altro, anzi ve lo domando in grazia di levarmi da queste pene con farmi prendere la mia robba e farmene ritornare alla mia patria, giacchè non ho potuto aver il piacere e l'onore di venir a ballare in questa città, dove era stato scritturato.

Appendix A

No. XXXIII.
Declaration of Luigi Berardi, *Dancer, July* 4, 1764. After waiting near a Month at Paris in vain expectation of money from *Giardini* to enable me to pursue my Journey, I got to London by the assistance of Signora *Tognoni* sent for by *Giardini* to sing there. On my arrival towards the end of January last, I was called upon by Signor *Sodi* in the name of *Giardini* to attend at the Rehearsal, and enter upon my business. I applied to *Giardini* from time to time for money on account of the pay I was entitled to by virtue of my Contract with Mr. *Leone, Giardini*'s Agent; but in vain. *Giardini* refused me any, and urged the invalidity of my Contract. Reduced to misery, in want of money, and Cloaths to appear in, he availed himself of my situation, to extort from me a fresh Contract, with a Deduction of about 45 £. *Sterl.* of my first Salary, which was for 200 Sequins. I was to be paid pro rata at so much a week. I have repeatedly applied to him for payment, and at this time he owes me about 20 £. *Sterl.* I declare this to be the Truth. July 4, 1764. Luigi Berardi.

No. XXXIV.[58]
Dear Sir, It is now five Months, that I have been living at Paris at my own expence. Not to trouble you with every minute particular, I shall only say, that I have made an exact calculation of my expences, which including the hire of my room, my eating and drinking, candles and fire when I was ill, amount to 3 Livres a day, which I must pay. You well know that I gave you at Lyons what money I had, so that on my arrival at Paris I was quite destitute. This has obliged me to pawn my Valise, my Music, my Watch, my Stone-Buckles, and even to my Boots. Consider then what I might have gained in all the time I have been here without employment, and labouring under a fit of Illness brought on by vexation. Relieve me, I earnestly beseech you, and enable me to redeem my Effects and return to my own Country, since I cannot have the honour of dancing in London according to my Contract. I entreat you to assist me. I am &c. Ravaschiello.

---

[55] Luigi Berardi (or Bararardi) danced at the Teatro S. Moisè at Venice in autumn 1763 with Maria Marcucci (see Wiel, p. 242). After joining the King's Theatre, Haymarket, in the spring of 1764 Berardi spent the season of 1764-65 at Drury Lane, where he was paid a respectable £2 per week. See *Biographical Dictionary*, II, 49 (where he is mistakenly said to have spent the season of 1763-64 at Drury Lane).
[56] Maddalena Tagnoni, Giardini's Third Woman for 1763-64.
[57] Ravaschiello (or Ravaschiollo) was the nickname of Vincenzo De Bustis. He danced at Venice in 1764-66 and again in 1769 at the S. Moisè, S. Benedetto and S. Giovanni Grisostomo theatres; at Reggio Emilia in 1771 and 1777 (where he was also choreographer); he danced again at Venice in 1775; and in 1779 at the Teatro Comunale at Bologna, always in comic operas.
[58] The following English version, from the *Réponse*, is a summary rather than a full translation.

Onde caro Amico e Padrone, la prego a volersi impegnare di ajutarmi ed anzioso de' vostri gentilissimi comandi me gli offerisco per sempre a servirla. Di V. S. Stimatissimo Signore Umilissimo servitore *Ravaschiello*

No. XXXV. Demarchis in Paris to Leone in London, 30 April 1764.
Cher Ami, Ho infine avuto il piacere di vedere e parlare al vostro raccomandatomi virtuoso *Ballerino* il Signor *Ravaschiello*, il quale in verità merita per la sua indole e buon carrattere ogni premura e attenzione da vostra parte e del Signor *Giardini*, avendo un'apoca ben legitima e ben formata senza la minima alterazione di verità. La situazione di questo povero giovane fa pietà, ed è sacrificato affatto, mentre per quel che deve per cinque mesi, gli hanno ritenuto e preso quanto gli era restato, come vedrete dalla sua nota, che vi includo; in conseguenza eccovelo in pieno in mezzo d'una strada con un talento non commune, mentre avendo ballato tre volte alla Commedia Italiana, senza però averne un soldo, ha sempre incontrato, ed è stato al sommo applaudito; Ma ciò non ha servito nè serve al povero giovane, che aumentargli affanni pene e afflizioni, che in fine l'hanno fatto cader malato. In conseguenza è troppo giusto e doveroso che in tale stato di cose, seriosamente voi ed il Signor *Giardini* pensiate a tirare e presto da guesto [sic] abisso di guai questo povero virtuoso, tanto più che onestamente altro non chiede che il denaro per ricuperare il suo, e solo 25 guinee per subito ritornarsene in Napoli, ove subito, non li mancherà impiego e pane. Assolutamente per onestà di voi altri due, dovete sollevare questo povero giovane, mentre vi sarebbe troppo disonore un trattamento sì barbaro verso un povero virtuoso tirato da un Teatro Reale, come voi *Caro Amico* ben sapete, il quale è giunto a darvi come ei mi dice fin quel poco resto di denaro che aveva in Lione, consistendo in dieci Zecchini tre luigi, e una doppia di Spagna. Caro per quanto vi sia cara la vostra integra probità, muovetevi a compassione di questo giovane, et fate ch'io possa riuscir con onore a quanto vi ho con verità esposto.

Voi conoscete Parigi; fa tremare per uno che sia in mezzo a una strada: mi dico Vostro fedele amico *Demarchis*.

No. XXXVI. Michel's Contract with Signora Marcucci, Bologna, 14 August 1763.
Con la presente privata scrittura, vogliono le parti, che abbiano forza come se fosse pubblico e giurato istrumento fatto da pubblico Notaro, si obbliga la Signora *Felice Marcucci*[59] di ballare in figura di prima grottesca col Signor *Pierre Bernard Michel*, che sarà il suo compagno nel Teatro di Londra, nel quale si fa ordinariamente le Opere, che principieranno al primo di Novembre 1763, e devono terminare alla fine di Giugno 1764. All'incontro si obbliga il Signor *Pierre Bernard Michel* pagare alla Signora *Felice Marcucci* 400 Zecchini, dico quattrocento Zecchini, e di più si obbliga il suddetto *Michel* condur la sud-

No. XXXV.
Dear Sir, I Have at last found out Mr. *Ravaschiello* the Dancer you recommended to me, who from his Talents and good Character merits every attention both from *Giardini* and yourself. His Contract appears just and legal, and his situation merits compassion: all his Effects are seized to pay his maintenance for five Months, as you will see by the Note I enclose. In consequence of this, his Talents cannot preserve him from the utmost misery. He has danced three times at the Italian Theatre, and met with the greatest applause; but as he received no pay, this has only served to aggravate his misfortunes, which at length have thrown him into a fit of Sickness. It is a duty incumbent on *Giardini* and you to extricate this worthy young Man out of his present situation. All he requests is wherewithal to redeem his Effects, and 25 Guineas to bear his expences to his own Country (Naples), where he will not long want employment. Absolutely for both your reputations you are bound to relieve him to prevent the imputation of Barbarity. You took him from a Royal Theatre, and, as he says himself, he gave you at Lyons what money he had left. You know Paris: it makes one tremble to see any Person driven to distress there; therefore as you value your own Character, shew some compassion for him. I am &c. Demarchis.

No. XXXVI.
By this private Writing, which the parties concerned agree shall have the same force as if it was an attested Instrument drawn up by a Notary Public, [Mrs] *Felice Marcucci* obliges herself to dance as first Comic Dancer with *Peter Bernard Michell*, at the Opera in London, which is to begin the first of November 1763, and continue till the end of June 1764. And *Peter Bernard Michell* obliges himself to pay the

---

[59] That is, Maria Marcucci, who danced with Luigi Berardi at Venice in autumn 1763.

detta con un'altra persona fino in Londra Libera di ogni spesa, e di pagar le rate conforme verranno pagate dall'Impresario di Londra salvo però i soliti Capi Teatrali. Io *Pierre Bernard Michel* affermo quanto sopra.

No. XXXVII. Carlo Graziani's statement, 5 September 1764.[60]

CIRCONSTANCES, *Dans lesquelles se trouvoit* M. Graziani *à Paris, lorsque* M. Giardini *l'a engagé à venir à Londres, & Particularités qui se sont passees entre eux depuis ce tems-là jusqu'à présent.*

A Peine fus-je arrivé à Paris, que je fus demandé par M. *de la Pouplinière* pour être premier Violoncelle de sa Musique, où j'ai demeuré jusqu'à sa mort avec des appointemens fort honnêtes & beaucoup au-dessus de ce qu'il avoit jamais donné à des Musiciens de cet Instrument. J'ai ensuite été attaché à M. *le Baron de Bocq*,[61] qui me donnoit les mêmes appointemens avec sa Parole d'honneur de me les constituer en Rente viagère. Pendant cette intervalle, je connus M. *Leone*, qui a demeuré quelques années à Paris, d'où il partit pour Londres. Comme j'avois été lié assez étroitement avec lui à Paris, j'entretenois sa correspondence d'autant plus volontiers, que j'étois bien aise de savoir si la reputation, que Londres s'est procurée dans toutes les Parties de l'Europe d'enrichir les Gens à Talent supérieur, étoit vraye ou fausse. M. *Leone* ne fit que m'entretenir par ses Lettres des grandes ressources & des avantages supérieurs qu'on y trouvoit, en me disant que mon séjour à Paris ne pouvoit que m'être désavantageux, & que tous les momens qui me séparoient de Londres, étoient des momens perdûs pour moi. Dans cette disposition, & bien avant le tems que j'eus la moindre relation avec M. *Giardini*, je lui marquai que, si par son crédit vis-à-vis ses amis il pouvoit m'assûrer quelque chose de fixe, je me déterminerois à me rendre à Londres. Cependant M. *Giardini* envoya le Sieur *Capitani*, Tailleur à Paris, avec ordre de me proposer la place de premier Violoncelle de son Opéra aux mêmes appointemens qu'avoit M. *Gordon*,[62] mon Prédécesseur, savoir une Guinée par soirée. Je m'étendis alors sur les avantages que je perdois en partant de Paris, & lui fis faire reflexion à la modicité de cette somme &c. Il me dit là-dessus qu'il en écriroit à M. *Giardini*, & qu'il me donneroit incessamment réponse. Quelque tems après je rencontrai le dit Sieur *Capitani* chez Mad. *Sartori*, qui me dit d'avoir écrit à M. *Giardini* les représentations que je lui avois faites, mais que je ferois bien de lui écrire aussi, & de lui faire entendre moi même mes intérêts. Je suivis ce conseil, & je marquai à M. *Giardini* que j'acceptois volontiers la Guinée par soirée qu'il me proposoit, mais qu'il payeroit mes voyages, & qu'il s'engageroit, comme je n'en doutois pas, à me procurer des Connoissances capables de me dédommager & de remplacer les bénéfices que je faisois à Paris. Apparamment il croyoit dans ce tems-là trop au-dessous de lui de me répondre directement; mais dans une entrevûe que j'eus

Appendix A

said [Mrs] *Felice Marcucci* four hundred Sequins, and to bear her expences, and also those of another Person with her to London free of all charges, and to pay her her Salary pro rata as he shall be paid by the Director of the Opera, the conditions usual in Theatres being understood. I *Peter Bernard Michell* affirm as above.

No. XXXVII.

The Circumstances of Mr [Carlo] Graziani in Paris when Mr Giardini engaged him to come to London, and details of what has passed between them from that time to the present.

Hardly had I arrived in Paris when M. de la Pouplinière invited me to become first cellist in his music, where I lived until his death with a very comfortable salary and much above what he had so far given musicians on that instrument. I have since been attached to Baron de Bagge, with the same salary and his word of honour for continuation for life. During this time, I made the acquaintance of Mr Leone, who lived for some years in Paris before leaving for London. Since I had been very close to him in Paris, I corresponded with him the more willingly as I was quite pleased to learn whether London's reputation throughout Europe for rewarding people of superior talent was true or not. In his letters Mr Leone led me to believe that there were many riches to be found there, telling me that my staying in Paris could only be to my disadvantage and that time away from London was time wasted. With this in mind and long before I had any contact with Mr Giardini, I indicated to [Leone] that if, through his influence with his friends, he could ensure some fixed income, I would resolve to take myself to London. Meanwhile Mr Giardini sent Signor Capitani, a tailor in Paris, with orders to offer me the place of first cello at his Opera under the same terms as my predecessor there, Mr Gordon—namely, a guinea per night. I then pointed out what I would lose in leaving Paris and reflected on the modest amount I was being offered. Thereupon, Capitani told me that he would write to Mr Giardini and let me have an immediate response. Some time later I met Signor Capitani at Madame Sartori's house, and he told me he had written to Mr Giardini outlining my conditions, but that I would do well to write to him and let him know my intentions myself. Following his advice, I indicated to Mr Giardini

---

[60] Carlo Graziani (d. 1787), though accidentally omitted from the *Biographical Dictionary*, was a composer and cellist of some distinction. See *New Grove*, VII, 654. This document adds a chapter to his biography. It appears to have been included in the *Réponse* as an afterthought, and no translation was printed. The one provided here is therefore our own. We have modernized titles of address in the French.

[61] That is, Baron Bagge. See note 40, above.

[62] John Gordon, fl. 1744-1773, member of the King's and Queen's bands. See *Biographical Dictionary*, VI, 275-276, where he is said probably to have been the Gordon who was a co-proprietor of the King's Theatre, Haymarket, from 1765 to 1773.

chez Mad. *Sartori* avec son Commissionnaire, celui-ci m'annonça qu'il étoit chargé de me dire très-expressément de la part de M. *Giardini*, qu'il étoit inutile de me mettre en peine d'aucune chose, de partir le plus-tôt que je pourrois, & d'être bien assuré sur sa parole qu'il m'accorderoit tout ce que je demandois, qu'il ne perdroit aucune occasion pour me rendre service, épouser mes intérêts, me recommander à toutes ses Connoissances, qu'en un mot je gagnerois plus de Guinées à Londres que je ne pouvois espérer de gagner d'Ecus à Paris.

Voilà l'aveu que me fit de sa part le Sieur *Capitani* en présence de Mad. *Sartori*, & je m'y fiai en aveugle d'autant plus volontiers que, rempli des sentiments de probité moi-même, je n'imaginois pas pouvoir connoître des hommes, sur qui cette probité n'avoit jamais eu le moindre accès. Je me disposai donc à mettre ordre à mes affaires pour partir, & dans le tems que je pensois le moins à être le premier à rendre service à M. *Giardini*, je vis entrer chez moi le Sieur *Capitani*, qui venoit d'un air empressé me prier de lui vouloir faire un plaisir important, qu'il devoit faire partir plusieurs Danseurs fugitifs, & qu'il n'avoit pas un Sol pour payer leur voyage, qu'ainsi il me prioit instamment au nom de M. *Giardini*, de vouloir lui prêter trente Louis d'or sur une Lettre de Change qu'il me donneroit, & qui me seroit remboursée à ma première entrevûe avec M. *Giardini*; enfin il me fit entendre qu'il ne pouvoit m'arriver une circonstance plus favorable pour me mettre en avance avec M. *Giardini* de tous les bons offices qu'il ne manqueroit pas de me rendre à Londres, & qui me conduiroient immanquablement dans le grand chemin de la fortune. Je me disposois à chercher une Chaise de Poste pour me rendre à Calais, lorsque je reçus une autre visite du Sieur *Capitani*, qui venoit pour m'insinuer que la Poste me couteroit fort cher, & cela pour me proposer une Berline de retour de Bologne, dans laquelle deux Danseurs partiroient avec moi, & qu'elle seroit très bien pour nous. Je voulus bien encore me laisser persuader, mais je ne m'attendois guères à la proposition qu'il me fit alors de vouloir bien fournir à ces Danseurs l'argent nécessaire pendant leur route, qui me seroit exactement rendu à mon arrivée par M. *Giardini*, en m'exaggérant toûjours les grandes obligations qu'on m'auroit. Je consentis à tout, & je m'envoiturai avec le Danseur, la Danseuse, & ma femme. On ne sauroit imaginer combien j'ai souffert de cette association pendant ma route, avec des Gens qui, n'ayant pas le Sol dans la poche, vouloient faire des dépenses de Seigneurs, s'imaginant que jusqu'aux brouillards de Londres tout y étoit d'or. J'ai eu encore presqu'autant à souffrir pour le remboursement de ces frais de voyage, qui ont néanmoins été payés demi Guinées à demi Guinées.

Dès mon arrivée, je me rendis chez M. *Giardini*, qui m'accabla de politesses; il ne me parut cependant pas si obligé que je l'aurois crû sur les avances que je lui avois faites à l'instigation du Sieur *Capitani*. Il me fit beaucoup de complimens sur mon talent, avant & après

my willingness to accept a guinea per night if he would pay my travel expenses and undertake, as I was sure he would, to arrange connections for me that would compensate me for the advantages I had in Paris. Apparently at that time he thought it beneath him to write to me personally, but in an interview I had at Madame Sartori's, his agent [Leone] told me that he was charged to tell me expressly on the part of Mr Giardini that it was pointless for me to be worried about anything, to set off as soon as possible, and to be completely assured by his word that he would grant me all that I was asking, that no opportunity would be missed to do me service, forward my interests, recommend me to all his acquaintances, that in a word I would earn more guineas in London than I could ever hope to earn écus in Paris.

This is the promise from him which Signor Capitani gave me in the presence of Madame Sartori, and I trusted in him blindly, never imagining that one could find men so devoid of any honesty. I then put my affairs in order ready to leave, little realizing that I would so soon be of service to Mr Giardini, when Signor Capitani entered my house eager to ask a favour: he had to get several runaway dancers ready to leave but had not a penny to pay for their trip; he begged me in the name of Mr Giardini to lend him 30 *Louis d'or* on a letter of credit that he would give me, and that I would be reimbursed at my first meeting with Mr Giardini; finally, he led me to believe that nothing more favourable could happen to me, by putting Mr Giardini in my debt, paving the way for all the favours he would doubtless do me in London, and that this would indubitably put me on the road to fortune. I was looking for a post-chaise for Calais, when I received yet another visit from Mr Capitani, who implied that the travelling post was too expensive and suggested that I take a 'Berline' [a kind of coach] returning to Boulogne, in which two dancers could travel with me, and that it would do very well for us. I let myself again be persuaded, but hardly expected that he should propose that I supply money to the dancers for their trip, which would be exactly refunded by Mr Giardini upon arrival. Exaggerating to myself how much this would ingratiate me [with Giardini] I agreed to everything, and I set off with the two dancers (male and female) and my wife. One cannot imagine how much I suffered en route from people who, without a penny in their pocket, wanted to live like lords, imagining that in London even the fog was made of gold. I have since suffered nearly as much by only being reimbursed half-guinea by half-guinea.

On my arrival, I paid a visit to Mr Giardini, who overwhelmed me with politeness. Nevertheless, he did not seem to be as grateful as I had been led to believe for the advances I had made at the instigation of Mr Capitani. He (Giardini) made me many compliments on my talent both before and after hearing me play. He wrote with many eulogies to Mr Soderini, a musician in Lord Pembroke's household, that here was the best cellist he had ever heard, and introduced me to Lord Pembroke and to Major Stainton, to whom I gave some

m'avoir entendu. Il écrit avec beaucoup d'éloge à M. *Soderini*,[63] Musicien chez Mylord *Pembrook*, qu'il avoit fait venir un Violoncelle supérieur à tous ceux qu'il avoit entendu, & il me procura la connoissance de Mylord *Pembrook* & de M. le Major *Stainton*, à qui j'ai donné des Leçons pendant l'Hyver. Je me soutins assés-bien avec lui pendant un certain tems, mais tout d'un coup, sans jamais en avoir sû la raison, il a commencé à se refroidir avec moi, & je n'ai jamais été plus surpris que de lui voir affecter certains airs d'hauteur & de mépris, qui ne vont jamais vis-à-vis d'un homme de bien, & d'apprendre qu'il ne perdoit aucune occasion pour décrier & mon talent & ma personne. En vérité, je n'avois jamais connu des caractéres qui ne vivent & ne s'abreuvent que de fiel!

Sur ce traitement j'eus avec lui des explications très-vives, & je le pressai de vouloir ranger les comptes entre nous, soit pour la Lettre de Change, dont j'ai presque reçu le montant, & que j'ai encore entre les mains, soit pour ce qui m'étoit dû de lui pour l'Opéra & pour les Concerts dans lesquels il m'a fait jouer, mais il m'a été impossible d'obtenir cet arrangement.

J'ai exactement marqué tout ce que j'ai reçu de M. *Giardini*, de son Frère & de son Trésorier, c'est de quoi on peut s'éclaircir sur mon Memoire.

Etat de ce qui est dû au Sieur Graziani *par M.* Giardini.

48 Représentations, à 1 £. 1 s.	50	8	0
Pour le Concert de Bénéfice de Mad. *Sartori*	3	3	0
Pour le Concert de Madame la Duchesse de *Graffton*	3	3	0
18 Concerts de Souscription	37	16	0
Pour mon Voyage de Paris à Londres	10	10	0
	105	0	0
Sur quoi j'ai reçû par M. *Giardini* ou par son ordre	44	2	0
Reste	60	18	0

Laquelle Somme 60 £. 18 s. M. *Giardini* sait bien lui-même qu'il me doit à très-juste tître.

Je Soussigné déclare, que le Memoire ci-dessus contient la pure vérité, & je consens qu'il soit imprimé avec celui de M. *Leone*. Londres, ce 5 de Sept. 1764. GRAZIANI.

Appendix A

lessons during the winter. For a while we remained on fairly good terms, but suddenly, without my having known the reason, he began to cool to me; and I was never so surprised as in finding him arrogant and scornful, which will never do towards a good man, and in learning that he never missed a chance to disparage my talent and my person. Truthfully, I had never before known any person who lived and thirsted for gall in such a fashion.

For this treatment I strongly expostulated with him, and I pressed him to settle the accounts between us, both for the letter of credit of which I have nearly received the total but which I still have in my hands, and for what he owes me for the opera and for the concerts in which he had me play, but it has been impossible to come to any accommodation.

I have indicated exactly what I have received from Mr Giardini, his brother and his treasurer, which can be found in the following statement.

Statement of what is due to Mr Graziani from Mr Giardini

48 [opera] performances at £1 1s	50	8	0
For the benefit concert for Madame Sartori	3	3	0
For the concert for the Duchess of Grafton	3	3	0
18 subscription concerts	37	16	0
For my trip from Paris to London	10	10	0
	105	0	0
I have received from Mr Giardini or by his order	44	2	0
Remainder	60	18	0

Mr Giardini well knows that he owes me the said sum of £60 18s.

I the undersigned declare that the memorandum above contains nothing but the truth, and I consent that it be published with that of Mr Leone. London, 5 September 1764. Graziani.

---

[63] Mr Soderini (fl. 1758-1794) was a violinist long active in London. See *Biographical Dictionary*, XIV, 193. His association with Lord Pembroke has not been known.

77

Appendix B

Leone's Contracts with Performers

Note: since the following contracts are highly formulaic, only the first two are given complete and verbatim. The rest include the substance of the contract, variations from the model provided by Giardini (see Appendix A, No. X) and any other distinctive details. Copytext for both Italian and English versions is C 12/521/4. Substantively identical copies of the English translations are also to be found in C 12/1008/4. Copies of the Mazziotti and Guglietti contracts in both languages are also recited in C 12/517/16.

I. Mazziotti's Contract, 22 September 1763

Per la presente benchè privata Scrittura da valere et aver forza come publico e giurato Istromento si dichiara da Noi sottoscritti D. Gabriele Leone Procuratore con speciale Mandato di Procura del Signor Felice Giardini Impressario del Real Teatro di Londra da una parte ed il Signor D. Antonio Mazziotti virtuoso cantante dall'altra qualmente per convenzione avuta fra di noi Io sottoscritto Mazziotti prometto e m'obligo ad ogn'ordine e richiesta di detto D. Gabriele partirmi da questa Città di Napoli e portarmi per le Poste nella Città di Londra senza far dimora in niuna Città di passaggio a riserba di qualche giorno per riposo e giunto sarò in detta Città di Londra prometto e m'obligo d'intervenire e cantare in qualita di prima parte nel sudetto Real Teatro in tutte le Opere Eroiche in Musica che si dovranno rappresentare in detto Teatro dal giorno del mio arrivo colà per tutto la fine di Giugno dell'anno entrante mille sette cento sessanta quatro con assistere in tutti li Concerti che per le medesime Opere occorreranno farsi di Giorno e di notte ed in qualunque altro luogo di detta Città ove parerà e piacerà a detto Signor Impressario e recitare in tutte le Serate d'opere senza limitazione di numero obbligandomi io sottoscritto Mazziotti di non mancare a quanto detto di sopra per qualsiasi Causa e Caso eccetto soltanto il caso di mia indisposizione (Iddio non voglia) nel qual caso sia tenuto detto Signor Impressario pazientarmi per giorni quindici quale elassi e non ritrovandomi ristabilito in salute sia al medesimo lecito durante la mia infermità pren-

Appendix B

I.

By this present Instrument Although Private as if it was a Publick and Sworn Instrument we the Underwritten Dr Gabriel Leone Special Attorney of Mr Felix Giardini Manager of the Royal Theatre in London on the one part and Mr Antonio Mazziotti singer of the other Part do hereby Declare that by an Agreement made between us the under Written Mazziotti do hereby promise and Oblige myself that when ever I shall be Ordered and required by the said Gabriel Leone I shall set out from the City of Naples to go by the post to the City of London without detaining my self in any of the Cities in my Voyage except some days to rest and as soon as I shall arrive in the City of London I do promise and Oblige myself to sing as first actor in the said Royal Theatre in all the Heroic Operas in Musick that shall be Acted in the said Theatre from the day of my Arrival there untill the End of June of the Ensuing year 1764 and shall attend in all the Concerts[1] that for the said Operas shall be made in the day time and at night and likewise in any other place of the said City where ever the Manager shall think proper and to act in all closing [sic] of the Operas without Limitation of Number Moreover I the said Mazziotti do Oblige myself not to fail to all what is above related upon any reason or cause whatsoever except in Case of my Indisposition (which God

---

[1] A mistranslation of 'Concerti'—i.e., rehearsals.

dere altro cantante in mio luogo con sodisfarlo per quel prezzo che si potrà convenire in danno di me sottoscritto Mazziotti All'incontro io sottoscritto D. Gabriele nel nome sudetto prometto e m'obligo far dare dà detto Impressario al sudetto Signor Mazziotti per onorario di sue virtuose fatiche faciende Zechini numero mille e cinque cento ò loro giusta valuta di Carlini ventisei l'uno moneta napoletana In conto e per Caparra del quale sudetto onorario Io sottoscritto Mazziotti dichiaro e confesso aver ricevuto dal' sudetto Signor D. Gabriele Zecchini trecento e li ristanti Zecchini Mille e due cento Io sottoscritto D. Gabriele m'obligo nel nome sudetto fare gli pagare in detta Città di Londra Mese per Mese pro rata m'obligo di più nel nome sudetto dare al sudetto Signor Mazziotti il viaggio per le Poste di andata e venire da questa Città di Napoli in quella di Londra ed a Londra a Napoli E m'obligo parimente far dare al sudetto Mazziotti una serata a suo beneficio a disposizione però del Signor Impressario in quella serata che li parerà e piacerà restando però a carico di detto Mazziotti di pagare lo spesato della medema Serata Obligandomi di non far mancare à quanto di sopra il detto Impressario per qualsiasi Causa eccetto soltanto ne casi d'incendio del Teatro ò divieto publico e simile nel qual caso debba il sudetto Signor Mazziotti esser pagatò à proporzione delle recite oltre dè sudetti intieri viaggi andare e venire come si costuma nè Teatri d'Italia in simili Congiuncture E finalmente conviene per patto espresso che mancando uno di noi una ò più volte ad'uno degl'articoli di sopra accordati di pagare all'altro ogni volta e per ciascuna controvenzione [a penalty sum seems to be missing here] obligamo per cio nei respettivi nomi sudetti le nostre Persone Napoli li 22 dico ventidue settembre mille cette [sette] cento sessanta tre 1763 Io Gabriele Leone Procuratore mi obligo come sopra Io Antonio Mazziotti mi obligo come sopra Io Saverio Mazziotti Padre del sudetto Antonio presto il mio consenso à quanto di sopra.

Ia. Guarantee of Mazziotti's Contract

Col presente Chirografo come se fosse publica Scrittura dichiamo che li Signor Morise e Caffarena publici Negozianti nella Città di Londra nostri corrispondenti con loro Lettera Missiva in data del ventisei del passato Agosto ci hanno commesso che avessimo qui assicurato l'onorarii di quei Soggetti che si sarebbero impegnati per mezzo di D. Gabriele Leone per la recita dovrà farsi colà in Londra in quel regio Theatro [sic] a tutto Giugno dell'anno entrante ed avendo detto Signor Leone Procuratore speciale del Signor Felice Giardini appaltato il Signor D. Antonio Mazziotti musico soprano per le recite

Appendix B

forbid) in which case the said Manager shall be Obliged to wait fifteen days but if after them I should not be reestablished in my health he shall be at Liberty during my Illness to take another Singer in my stead paying him what price he can agree for at the Cost of me the underwritten Mazziotti and I the under Written Dr. Gabriel [Leone] of the other part in the Name of the above mentioned do oblige myself that the said Manager shall pay the said Mazziotti for Salary for his virtuous trouble one thousand five hundred Sequins or their true Value of twenty six Carlini each of Neapolitan Currency and I the under Written Mazziotti do hereby declare and acknowledge that I have received on Account and for earnest of my said Salary three hundred Sequins and I the under Written Dr. Gabriel do oblige myself in the name of the above said that the remaining Twelve hundred Sequins shall be paid to him in the said City of London by Monthly Payments month by month pro rata and further I do oblige myself in the Name of the abovesaid to pay him the said Mazziotti for his Voyage going by the post from this City of Naples to that of London and from London to Naples and further do oblige myself that said Manager shall grant to the said Mazziotti a Benefit Night but on what Night shall be thought proper the said Mazziotti shall be obliged to pay the Charges of the said Night and further do Oblige myself that the said Manager shall not fail all that has been abovesaid upon any account whatsoever excepting only if the Theatre shall be burnt or a Publick prohibition for [sic] the like in which case the said Mr Mazziotti shall be paid in proportion for what he shall have Acted besides the whole Voyage of his going and Coming as it is Customary in the Theatres in Italy on the like Accidents and lastly we have agreed expressly that if any of us should be wanting once or more times to any of the above Articles agreed on to pay one unto the other every time and for every Controversy [C 12/1008/4 reads: controvertion] (the Damage that the same shall Occasion) to which we oblige our persons in the respective names aforesaid Naples 22d September 1763 I Gabriel Leone Attorney oblige myself as above I Antonio Mazziotti Oblige myself as aforesaid I Saverio Mazziotti ffather of Antonio Aforesaid give my Consent to the above.

Ia.

By this Present Instrument as if it was a Publick Instrument we do declare that Messrs. Morris and Cafferena of the City of London Merchants our Correspondents by their Letter Dated the 26th of August last past have Ordered that we should be Security here for the Salarys of such persons that should Engage themselves by Means of Mr Gabriel Leone for to Act in the Operas that shall be Acted in the Royal Theatre in London until the End of the Month of June in the ensuing year and the said Mr Leone Special Attorney of Mr Felice Giardini having Engag'd Mr Antonio Mazziotti an excellent Musician to Act

81

sudette a tutto il sudetto tempo per l'onorario tra di loro convenuto di Zecchini mille e duecento di Carlini ventisei l'uno moneta napoletana oltre il viaggio di andata e ritorno per le poste franco come dalla Scrittura Passata questo presente giorno tra detti Signori Mazziotti e Leone in detto nome Onde per essecuzione della sudetta Lettera la sottoscritta nostra compagnia seu ragione cantante [contante?] Wills e Leigh nel dilei seu nostro proprio nome assicura seu assicuramo al sudette Signor Mazziotti detto suo onorario di Zecchini mille e duecento ed importo di detti viaggi di andata e ritorno obligandoci quelle pagare allo stesso Signor Mazziotti in tutto ò in parte quallora dà detto Signor Giardini ò da altri in nome di quello non fusse sodisfatto di detto onorario e viaggi accordatili à tenore della sudetta Scrittura d'appaldo quel pagamento promettemo fare coll'esibizione della medesima Scrittura e colla fede giurata di esso Signor Mazziotti della quantità che restasse forze [forse] à consequire senza che noi possiamo addurre contro detto pagamento eccezzione alcuna se non che l'esibizione della ricevuta in forma valida dello stesso Signor Mazziotti e particolarmente senza poter addurre che si debba prima discutere in caso di [man]canza col Signor Felice Giardini Impressario come principale obbligato intendendo che resti la nostra Compania obbligata ad esso Signor Mazziotti anche come principale obligata ed inmentre attento questa nostra cautela esso Signor Mazziotti si è indetto a partire per Londra a far dette recite e perciò promettemo dare (in detto caso) essecuzione alla presente Cautela da noi fattoli con dichiarazione che oltre li sudetti Zecchini mille e duecento da noi assicurati detto Signor Mazziotti ha recevuto anticipamente in questa Città altri Zechini trecento per mano del detto Signor Leone Obligando per l'effetto sudetto le nostre persone seu la detta nostra ragione nostri Eredi Successori e Beni tutti presenti e futuri colla clausola del Costo precario e giuramento in Forma Napoli li 22 Settembre 1763 Wills & Leigh E in fede della sopra detta firma Io Notaio Liberio Scæla di Napoli ho segnata Scæla.

II. Baini's Contract, 22 September 1763

In nomine Dei amen per la presente privata Scrittura da Valere e Tenere come se fosse un publico giurato Istromento apparisca qual mente la Signora Cecilia Baini si obliga di ritrovarsi in Londra per [blank] ed ivi trattenersi fino a tutto il Mese di Guigno 1764 e durante detto Tempo intervenire e cantare a tutte e quante quelle prove e recite dell'Opere che si faranno nel Real Teatro e che le saranno ordinate del Signor Felice Giardini direttore di detta opera dippiù si obliga la sudetta Signora Cecilia Baini con suo Marito il Signor Antonio Baini di non cantare in veruna Assemblea o Luogo fuori dell' Opera senza prima averne ottenuta la permissione in scritto dal detto Signor Giardini e mediante le sudette Condizioni il sudetto Signor Felice Giardini si obliga di pagare al sudetto e sudetta per le loro

as aforesaid during the time above mentioned at and for the Salary by them Agreed of Twelve hundred Sequins of 26 Carlines each Neapolitan Currency besides the Expences of the Voyages of going and Coming by the Post as appears by the Instrument made this present day between Messrs. Mazziotti and Leone in the said name [of Felice Giardini?] therefore in pursuance of the said Letter (our said Company runing [sic] by the Names of Wills and Leigh) that is to say we do assure to the said Mr Mazziotti his said Salary of Twelve hundred Sequins as likewise the amount of the Expences of the said Voyages of going and coming Obliging ourselves to pay the same to the said Mr Mazziotti in all or part whenever the said Mr Giardini or others in his Name should not pay the said salary and Expences of the Voyages agreed upon according to the said Instrument of Engagement which Payment we promise to make whenever the said Instrument shall be Exhibited with an Affidavit of the said Mazziotti declaring the quantity that shall so remain unpaid without our Alledging against the said Payment any Exception whatever but with the Exhibition of the Receipt in due fform of the said Mr Mazziotti and particularly without Alledging that in Case of ffailure Mr Felix Giardini the Manager should be first Consulted as Principal Debtor willing that or [our?] Company shall be obliged to the said Mr Mazziotti as Principal Debtor and in Consequence of this our Security the said Mr Mazziotti agreed to go to London to Act as aforesaid and therefore he promised to give in Case that Execution to this present Security by us so given him declaring here in that on Account of the One thousand two hundred Sequins by us insured the said Mazziotti has received in Advance in this City Three hundred Sequins by the hands of Mr Leone for the Purposes abovesaid our persons that is to say our said Company our Heirs Successors and Goods all present and future with the Clause Costo precario and Oath in Form Naples the 22d Sepr. 1763. Wills & Leigh In Witness of the above Signature I Libario Scæla of Naples Notary have signed Scæla.

II.

In Dei Nomine Amen by this present private Writing of equal force and Obligation as if it was a Publick sworn Instrument it appears that Mrs. Cecilia Baini Obliges herself to Repair to London and to remain there till the End of the month of June 1764 and during the said time to be present and to sing at all and as many Rehearsals and Representations of Operas as shall be made at the Theatre Royal and shall be Ordered by Mr Felice Giardini Manager of the Opera moreover the above mentioned Siga. Cecilia Baini Obliges herself with her Husband Signor Antonio Baini not to sing at any Assembly or place whatsoever except the Opera without having first previously Obtained Leave in Writing of the said Signor Giardini and on this Condition the aforesaid Signor Felice Giardini Obliges himself to pay to the said

virtuose fatiche Zechini cinquecento o loro Valuta in tutto e dovendo cantare da prima Donna darli cento Zechini di più e detta paga in due rate la metà dopo le venticinque recite ed il rimanente alla fine della staggione intendendosi che ne casi d'Incendio di Teatro divieto publico e simili il sudetto e sudetta debba esser pagato a proporzione delle recite e come si costuma nè Teatri d'Italia in simili Congiunture e finalmente li sudetti Felice Giardini e Signora Cecilia Baini concordemente e di reciproco consenzo convengono che quello di loro controverrà una o più volte ad uno o più degl'articoli di sopra accordati pagherà all'altra ogni volta e per ciascheduna controvenzione la pena di Zecchini cento oltre al rifacimento de danni, le quali pene e danni dovranno esser computati in conto di paga in oltre il sudetto Signor Giardini si obbliga anticipare a conto dell'onorario la summa di cento cinquanta Zechini in fede di che questa con altra simile sarà segnata da ambe le parte come per una parte del detto contratto segnato per il detto Gabriel Leone

III. Guglietti's Contract, 28 September 1763

Per la presente benchè privata Scrittura . . . Il Signor D. Domenico Guglietti virtuoso Cantante . . . partirmi da questa Città di Napoli e portarmi per le Poste nella Città di Londra senza far dimora in niuna Città di passaggio à riserba di qualche giorno per riposo . . . promitto e mi obbligo intervenire e cantare nel sudetto Real Teatro dà quella parte che parerà à detto Impresario in tutte le opere Eroiche in Musica . . . assistere in tutti li Concerti che per le medesime opere occorretanno farsi di giorno e di notte in Teatro et in qualunque altro luogo . . . soltanto il Caso dì mia Indisposizione (Iddio non voglia) nel qual Caso sia tenuto detto Impresario pazientare per Giorni quindeci quali elassi e non ritrovandomi ristabilito in salute sia al medesimo lecito durante la mia Infirmità prendere altro Cantante in mio Luogo . . . per onorario di sue virtuose fatiche faciende Zechini numero quattro cento . . . farceli pagare in detta Città di Londra Mese per Mese pro rata . . . il Viaggio di andata per le Poste da . . . Napoli in quella di Londra ed il viaggio di ritorno . . . .

Signor Antonio Baini and Cecilia Baini for their Theatrical Labor five hundred Sequins or the Value thereof in all and in case she shall be Employed as first woman Singer to give her One hundred Sequins more and the above Salary to be paid in two payments the one half after Twenty five Exhibitions and the other half at the End of the Season provided and on Condition [that if] the Theatre should be burnt down or that there should be a prohibition from Acting or any like case and in such Case the said Signor Antonio Baini and the said Cecilia Baini shall be paid in proportion to their Labour in Representing and as it is Customary in the Theatres in Italy in like cases and finally the said Signor Felice Giardini and the said Cecilia Baini do unanimously and by reciprocal Consent Agree that either of them who shall fail once or more times to one or more of the Above Articles as agreed to shall pay to the other each time and for every Breach the Penalty of One hundred Sequins besides Reparation of Damages the which penalty and Damages shall be Computed in lieu or part of payment and further the said Signor Giardini Obliges himself to Anticipate upon Account of their Salary the Sum of One hundred and fifty Sequins In Witness . . . .

III.

By this present Instrument . . . Mr Dominico Guglietti Singer . . . do hereby Promise and Oblige myself . . . I Shall set out from the City of Naples to go by the post to the City of London . . . and Oblige my self to Sing in the . . . Royal Theatre in that part that the Manager shall think most Proper in all the Heroic Operas in Musick . . . and shall attend in all the Concerts [i.e., rehearsals] that for the said Operas shall be made in the day time and at the Theatre at night . . . and to Act in all Closing [sic] of the Operas without Limitation of Number . . . except in Case of my Indisposition . . . in which case the said Manager shall be Obliged to Wait fifteen days but after them if I should not be be established in my health he shall be at Liberty . . . to take another Singer in my stead Paying him what Price he can agree for at the Cost of me . . . the said Manager shall Pay the said Guglietti for Salary for his Virtuous Trouble four hundred Sequins . . . I have received on Account and for earnest of my said Salary 100 Sequins . . . [Leone promises] that the remaining 300 Sequins shall be paid to him in the City of London by Monthly payments Month by month Pro rata and further I do Oblige my self in the name of the Abovesaid to pay . . . Guglietti for his Voyage going by the Post from . . . Naples to . . . London and for his Voyage in Returning to . . . Naples and further do Oblige my self that the said Manager shall not fail of all what has been above said Upon Any Account whatsoever excepting only that if the Theatre be burnt . . . in which case the said Mr Guglietti shall be paid in proportion of what he shall have Acted besides the whole Voyage of his going and coming . . . Naples 28th Sepr. 1763.

IV. Marcucci's Contract, 26 October 1763

In dei Nomine Amen Venezia . . . Con la presente benchè privata scrittura . . . la Signora Felice [sic] Marcucci si obliga di venire in Londra in Compagnia del Signor Gabriele Leone incaricato di Procura da Signor Felice Giardini . . . franca di ogni speza del Viaggio ed ivi a tal effetto ballare sino alla fine di Giugno 1764 in qualità di prima Grottesca cioè a di ne Padedu [pas de deux], Terzetti, Quartetti e Durante questo Tempo intervenire a tutte e quante quelle prove che li saranno dal . . . Giardini ordinate obbligandozi in ricompenze delle sue virtuose fatiche di accordarli la summa di Zecchini quattrocento cinquanta Veneti . . . Leone pagarli anticipatamente a Lione ed il rimanente farli pagare dal sudetto . . . Giardini in Londra mese per mese pro Rata . . . la penalità di cento Zecchini . . . .

V. Vento's First Contract, undated [late August or September 1763][2]

In Dei Nomine amen Per la presente privata Scrittura da valere e tenere come se fosse un publico giurato Istrumento apparisca qualmente il Signor Mattia Vento si obliga di ritrovarsi in Londra per il principio di Novembre ed ivi trattenersi fino a tutto il mese di Giugno 1764 e durante detto Tempo intervenire e comporre due opere che si faranno nel Real Teatro nel tempo che le saranno prescritte dal Signor Felice Giardini direttore di detta Opera dippiù si obliga il suddetto di assistere a tutte le prove e recite che nelle sue opere si faranno e mediante le sudette conditioni il sudetto Signor Giardini si obliga di pagare al Signor Mattia Vento per le sue virtuose fatighe Zechini trecento in tre volte cioè cento Zecchini anticipati per la fine di Settembre ed il rimanente cento in ciascuna opera che il sudetto Signor Mattia [Vento] dovrà comporre intendendosi che nè casi d'incendio di Teatro divieto publico simile debba esser pagato a proporzione delle sue virtuose fatighe e come si costuma ne Teatri de Italia in simile congionture e finalmente li sudetti Felice Giardini e Signor Mattia Vento concordemente e di reciproco consenso convengono che quello di loro contraverrà una o più volte all'articoli di sopra accennati pagherà all'altro ogni volta e per ciascheduna controvenzione la pena che sarà computata in conto di Paga che da persone experte sarà il tutto Giudicato ed in Fede di che questa con altra simile sarà segnata da ambe le parti Io Gabriele Leone per Felice Giardini Io Leopoldo Castelli fui testimonio

---

[2] Date from C12/521/4 (answer of Vento).

Appendix B

IV.

Venice . . . By the present Writing . . . Mrs Felice Marcucci Obliges herself to go to London with Mr Gabriel Leone . . . free of all Expences of her Journey and to Dance there to the End of June 1764 In Quality of first Comic Woman Dancer that is to say in the Step of two three four and during this time to be present at all and every Rehearsal directed by the said ffelice Giardini he Obliging himself as a Reward for all her pains and Trouble to pay her the Sum of four hundred and fifty Sequins of Venice or their Value One hundred of which the said Gabriel Leone Obliges himself to Advance her at Lyons the rest to be paid her by the said Felice Giardini in London monthly per Month pro Rata. . . . Wherefore the Parties Cordially and by reciprocal Consent agree that which ever of them shall fail in any one of these Articles one or more times agreed on shall pay to the other as a Penalty One hundred Sequins which in Case of failure shall be Computed on Account of pay. . . .

V.

In Dei Nomine Amen By the present writing . . . Mr Mattia Vento Obliges himself to be in London by the Beginning of November and there to remain till the very End of the Month of June 1764 and during that Time to come and compose two Operas to be represented in the Royal Theatre at the time it shall be ordered him by Mr Felice Giardini director of the said opera Moreover the abovesaid obliges himself to assist at all the Rehearsals and Recitals which shall be made of his operas and on these Conditions the said Mr Felice Giardini obliges himself to pay to Mr Mattia Vento for his pains and trouble three hundred Sequins at three Times that is to say one hundred Sequins in Advance by the End of September and the Remainder one hundred for each Opera that the said Mr Mattia Vento shall compose it being understood that in Case of the Theatre's being on Fire which shall become publick[3] and the like he shall be paid in proportion to his pains and as is customary in the Theatres in Italy . . . lastly the said Felice Giardini and Mr Mattia Vento cordially and by mutual Consent agree that which ever of them shall fail . . . shall pay to the other for each failing and each nonperformance the penalty which shall be computed on account of Pay and which shall be adjudged by expert persons In Testimony of which this with a Duplicate shall be signed by both parties.

---

[3] The text is evidently defective here in both C12/521/4 and C12/1008/4. Most of the text about prohibition of acting on account of the death of princes is missing.

VI. Vento's Second Contract, undated [c mid-December 1763][4]

In Dei Nomine Amen Per la presente benchè privatta scrittura da valere e tenere come se fosse un publico giurato Istromento apparisca qualmente il Signor Mattia Vento si obliga di ritrovarsi in Londra per la metà de 8bre [ottobre] 1763 ed ivi comporre un opera per il regio Teatro ed intervenire e sonare a tutte quante quelle prove che saranno necessarie in dett'opera ed ordinate dal Signor Felice Giardini Direttore del Regio Teatro per il prezzo di Zecchini ducento venti e se accaso il Signor Felice Giardini volesse che nella Stagione scrivesse un altera Opera sia lo stesso Signor Felice Giardini obbligato di pagarli dippiù del primo accordo altri ottanta Zechini che per tal effetto e di reciproco consenzo convengono che quello di loro contraverra una o più volte ad uno o più degl'Articoli di sopra accordati sarà sottoposto alle pene e rifacimento de danni le quali pene e danni dovranno esser computati in conto di paga in fede di che questa con altra simile sarà segnata da ambe le parti Io Gabriel Leone per Felice Giardini Gennaro Biasco Celestini fui presente come per un duplicato del istesso contratto segnato del detto Gabriel Leone e adesso nella possessione. . . .

---

[4] Date from C 12/517/16.

Appendix B

VI.

In the Name of God Amen . . . Be it known That Mr Mattia Vento obliges himself to be at London by the Middle of October 1763 where he is to compose an Opera for the Royal Theatre and to [C 12/1008/4 adds: be present and] play at all and whatever Rehearsals of the said Opera which shall be necessary and shall be ordered by Mr Felix Giardini Manager of the said Royal Theatre for the price of two hundred and twenty Zequins And if Mr Felix Giardini shall require that during the Season he shall write another Opera then and in such Case he the said Mr Giardini is obliged to pay him besides the first agreement eighty zequins more and to which Effect and by Reciprocal Covenant the parties do hereby agree that if any of them shall be wanting once or more times in any of the above articles agreed on [they] shall be obliged to pay the penalty and make good the damage which penalty and damage shall be reckoned on account of payment In Witness whereof this with another of the same Tenor shall be signed by both parties Gennaro Biasco Celestini was present. I Mattia Vento Attest as above I Gabriel Leone for Felix Giardini.

Index

Agos, Joseph, 50
Alessandro nell'Indie: See Bach and Cocchi
Anderson, Emily, 27
Armida abbandonata: See Jommelli
Arnott, James Fullarton, vii
Asselain, Mlle, 52-53
Atri (Teramo), 56
Augusta, Princess, 15, 60
Auretti, Janneton: on King's Theatre roster for 1763-64, 13; retained for 1764-65, 28

Bach, Johann Christian, vi, 14, 19: *Alessandro nell'Indie*, 45; brought to London in 1762, 2; leaves England, 3, 48; *Orione*, 3, 57; quarrel with Manzuoli made up, 28; return to Continent in 1763, 3; returns to London in 1764, 28; *Zanaida*, 3, 57
Bagge, Baron, 52-53, 56, 72: gives Giardini unwanted advice, 18
Baglioni, Francesco, 45
Baglioni, La, 44
Bagniani, Carmine, 9
Baini, Antonio, 82: receipt to Leone, 66
Baini, Cecilia, 66: contract with Leone, 82; criticized by Mingotti and Giardini, 8-9; husband's receipt to Leone, 66; in King's Theatre roster for 1763-64, 12; paid £40 by Rich, 25; party to lawsuit, vi, 21; petitions to testify in Italian, 26; salary advance, 20; serves as *ultima parte*, 10; signed by Leone, 8
Balducci, Rosalba, 56
Barazzi, Francesco: letter to Leone, 66
Barcelona, 12
Baretti, Giuseppe, 17, 38-39
Basso, Alberto, viii
Berardi, Luigi, 11, 71: accused of loitering in Paris, 11; claims against Giardini bought, 22; declaration of grievances, 68; marries Tagnoni, 25; on King's Theatre roster for 1763-64, 13; salary advance, 20
Bernacchi, Antonio Maria, 40
Bernardi: See Berardi
Bertoni, Ferdinando, 53
Bianchi, Marianna, 46
Bologna, 5, 8, 11, 40, 52, 56: Teatro Comunale, 45, 47, 69
Bottarelli, Giovanni, 15
Boulogne, 74
Brame, Giuseppe, 62
Brito, Manuel Carlos de, 25
Brivio, Giuseppe Ferdinando, 5, 38: proposes Cateneo, 40; recommends

Bianchi, 46
Bromfield, Mr (doctor), 48
Brucciatina, La: See Spagnioli, Clementina
Brunswick, Prince of, 7, 15
Brussels, 56
Buckingham, Samuel von, 21
buona figliuola, La: See Piccinni, Niccolò
Buonsollazzi: See De Amicis
Burney, Charles: assessment of Vento's music, 19; error about Mingotti, 3; on 'inauspicious' 1763-64 season, 7; praise for Giardini as violinist, 1; praise for Guarducci, 40
Burnim, Kalman A., viii

Cacophron: See Rich, Sir Robert
Caffarena, Signor, 46, 50, 54: see also, Morris and Caffarena
Calais, 52, 74
Capitani, Joseph, 46, 74: cozens Graziani into helping with travel expenses, 74; helps recruit Graziani in Paris, 72; identity and distress benefit, 13; King's Theatre tailor for 1763-64, 13
Capitani, Polly, 13, 53-54
Caruso (cellist?), 50
Cattaneo, Antonio, 5, 10, 38, 64: salary demands, 40
Cattilini, Giacomo, 6, 40-41, 56: maximum salary to be offered, 40
Celestini, Gennaro Biasco, 20, 25
Cerocchi: See Pozzi
Chamberont, Matteo, 44
Cocchi, Gioacchino, 2: *Alessandro nell'Indie*, 9
Combe, Signor, 66
Consoli, Tommaso, 44
Consolini, 44, 46
contracts: form, 42; Giardini's alleged right to ratify, 19; penalties, 44; with minors, 44; see also, dancers and individual performers
Conway, Henry Seymour, 7
Cornelys, Mrs: concert room, 17
Crawford, Peter, 2: announces retirement from management, 2; return to management reported, 28
Cremonini, Clementina: engaged as *ultima parte*, 10; father refuses to sign her contract, 64; hired by Giardini, 48, 50; joins company in 1764-65, 28; signed by Giardini as third woman, 5; solicits offer from Giardini, 48
Crosa, Giovanni Francesco, 1: goes into exile, 2
Cucuel, G., 53

90

Index

dancers: Berardi's affidavit, 68; De Bustis' complaint, 68; Giardini's instructions for hiring, 10-12, 52; Leone's contract with Marcucci, 86; Leone's negotiations with, 10; Magri on dancers' terms, 54; Marcucci demoted to figurante, 12; Michel's contract with Marcucci, 70; negotiations for Dauberval, 28; roster for 1763-64, 13; salary scale for, 27; the Varanellis to be considered, 44; see also, Berardi, De Bustis, Formigli, Magri, Maranesi, Marcucci, Michel

Dauberval, Jean Bercher: extravagant offer for services of, 28; on King's Theatre roster for 1763-64, 13

Davide, Giacomo, 10

De Amicis, Anna Lucia, 56-57

De Amicis, Domenico, 56

De Amicis, Domenico Antonio, 56

De Angelis, A., 37

De Bustis, Vincenzo, 12: Demarchis' letter about, 70; hired by Leone, 11; salary advance, 20; statement of grievances, 68

de la Pouplinière: See Riche de la Pouplinière, Le

Defence of F. Giardini, vii: explanation of feud with Rich, 24; on creditors' meeting, 22

Demarchis, Mons., 70

Didone abbandonata: See Piccinni

Drummonds Bank, v, 22, 27

Dublin, 52

Duvall, Mr: on King's Theatre roster for 1763-64, 13

Egiziano, L': See Vento

Elisi, Filippo, 48-49

Enea e Lavinia: See Giardini

Farinelli [Carlo Broschi], 8, 40

Farmer, Mr, 50, 54: see also, Fermier

Fermier, Mr, 28

Fermo, 56

Festing, Michael Christian, 1

finta giardiniera, La: See Mozart, W. A.

Fishar, James: on King's Theatre roster for 1763-64, 13

Florence, 19, 41, 44, 62

Florimo, F., 37

Formigli, Maddalena ('La Mora'), 11, 56

Fortescue, Sir John, 23

Francavilla, Prince of, 8

Genoa, 8, 44

George III, 7, 15, 58

Giardini, Felice: accused of cheating Berardi, 68; accuses Leone of dallying with women, 62; admits debt to Graziani, 25; advice on avoiding customs duty, 20, 60; allowable augmentations to salaries, 42; apology to Leone for credit problems, 56; aria used in *Leucippo*, 16; attempts to placate creditors, 23; bank account overdrawn, 22; called Piemontesino, 38; calls Baini a bad singer, 9; calls meeting of creditors, 22; cavalier view of contracts, 18; Chancery countersuit against, 22; charges Leone with taking kickbacks, 7; co-manager in 1756-57, 2; complaint in *Public Advertiser*, vi, 22; composes English catch, 25; concert with Graziani, 25; confined to house by debts, 23; debts bought up by Rich, 25; decision to concentrate on *opera seria*, 2; departure from management reported, 27; desire to mount *opera seria*, 26; disorganization of, 5; *Enea e Lavinia*, 21-22; forbids payment of travel and lodging expenses, 40; goods acquired for by Leone in Italy, 20; hires Giustinelli and Cremonini, 48; in financial straits by March 1764, 21; leader of band for 1763-64, 13; letter of attorney to Leone, 38; letter of credit for Leone to Mme Grasse, 46; loses patience with Leone, 18; music copied for, 20; obtains Chancery injunction, 22; on urgent need for bass, 64; on urgent need for *ultima parte*, 64; orchestral player and manager in 1750s, vi; payments to Leone, 19; Piedmontese dialect, 36; praised by Burney as violinist, 1; proposed salary scale for 1763-64, 40; provides general contract form, 42; receives opera license in 1763, vi; reported bankrupt by Leopold Mozart, 27; solicits 1763-64 subscription, 3; statement of money owed to Graziani, 76; states contract penalties, 44; states Ten Commandments, 4, 42; suit against performers, vi; to blame for failure of season, 19; unsuccessful arbitration offer, 23; view of pasticcio, 15; 1770 concert series with Vento, 17

Gibbons, Orlando, 25

Gibson, Elizabeth, v, 22, 27

Giordani, Nicolina (called La Spiletta), 23

Giovanetti, Pietro, 10: Assistant Manager for 1763-64, 13; letter to Leone, 64

Giustinelli, Giuseppe, 26, 52, 54, 56, 58: goes to Lisbon for 1765-66, 25; hired by Giardini, 48, 50; in King's Theatre roster for 1763-64, 12; kept dangling by Giardini, 48; salary unknown, 27; signed by Giardini as second man, 5

Gluck, Christoph Willibald: *Alceste*, 57; *Orfeo*, 47

Goldoni, Carlo, 26

Gordon, John, 25, 72-73

Gower, Lord, 28

91

Grasse, Mme, 4, 44, 46, 54
Graziani, Carlo, 25, 58: concert with Giardini, 25; principal cellist for 1763-64, 13; statement of grievances against Giardini, 72; statement of money owed to him by Giardini, 76; to be offered a place in the orchestra, 54; to be paid a guinea a night, 72
Grimaldi (impresario in Venice), 12
Guadagni, Gaetano, 41
Guadagnin (identity uncertain), 40
Guadagnini, Giovanni Battista, 41
Guarducci, Tommaso, 6, 50: demands £1000 salary, 27; salary demands, 40
Gubbio, 8
Guglielmi, Pietro Alessandro, 53
Guglietti, Domenico: contract with Leone, 84; engaged by Leone, 9; explains kickback scheme, 21; in King's Theatre roster for 1763-64, 12; nature of employment at King's Theatre, 9; paid £23 by Rich, 25; party to lawsuit, vi, 21; petitions to testify in Italian, 26; salary advance, 20

Handel, G. F., 14
Harris, James, Earl of Malmesbury, 27
Harris, Mrs, 27
Hasse, Johann Adolf, 16
Hertford, Earl of, 7
Highfill, Philip H., viii
Hoffman, E. T. A., 53
Holland, 56
Holmes, W. C., 26
Huet, Mme, 44

Jerney and Merry, 62
Jommelli, Niccolò: *Armida abbandonata*, 57

LaLauze, Miss: on King's Theatre roster for 1763-64, 13
Langhans, Edward A., viii
Leone, Gabriele: alleged author of *Réponse*, vi; cavalier view of contracts, 18; claims to have lost Vento's contract, 16; claims 6-guinea weekly salary as musician, 21; dallies with Roman women, 18; defends Vento's salary, 16; dishonesty of, 5; engages Mazziotti as first man, 6; hired as agent by Giardini, 3; letter of attorney from Giardini, 38; money received and expended on trip, 19; party to lawsuit, vi, 21; petitions to testify in Italian, 26; problems financing travels, 4; receipt of kickbacks, 21; recruits Graziani in Paris, 72; remuneration of, 20; reply in *Public Avertiser*, vi; ships goods to Giardini, 20; signs Baini, 8; signs Vento's first contract, 86; signs Vento's second contract, 88; unsatisfactoriness as agent, 19

Lewis, W. S., viii
Lisbon, 25, 52
London, 1-5: Covent Garden Theatre, 8, 23, 52; Drury Lane Theatre, 23, 48, 52; King's Bench, 22; King's Theatre, Haymarket, v, vii, 1-2, 10, 14, 22-23, 25-26, 40, 45, 48-49, 52, 56, 60, 66, 69, 73, 78, 80, 82, 84, 86; £2000 deficit in 1763, 2; 1764 takeover attempt, 25; Public Record Office, vi, 37; Sadler's Wells Theatre, 12; Spring Garden, 48
Lord Chamberlain, 1, 23, 28
Luciani, Domenico, 6, 40: demands £1500 salary, 27; salary demands, 40; to be paid up to 1800 zecchini, 40
Lucio Silla: See Mozart, W. A.
Lyons, 4, 19, 66

Maddaloni, Duke of, 8
Madrid, 40
Magri, Gennaro, 10: letter to Leone, 11, 54; *Trattato teorico-prattico di ballo*, 11, 55
Manziotti: See Mazziotti
Manzuoli, Giovanni, 23, 46: pleases subscribers in 1764-65, 28; quarrel with Johann Christian Bach made up, 28; receives £1500 guaranteed salary, 27
Maranesi, Cosimo, 11, 52
Marchesio (Marchisio), Giuseppe, 44, 46, 54, 64
Marcucci, Maria, 11-12: accompanies Leone to London, 5; contract with Leone, 86; contract with Michel, 70; dances with Berardi, 69; demoted to figurante and goes to Sadler's Wells, 12; engaged by Leone, 11; hissed at King's Theatre, 12; on King's Theatre roster for 1763-64, 13; paid £5 by Rich, 25; party to lawsuit, vi, 21; petitions to testify in Italian, 26; replaced by Auretti, 28; salary advance, 20
Martini, Padre Giovanni Battista, 5, 38
Mattei, Colomba, 2, 46: leaves England, 3, 48; plans to leave England, 2
Maurò, Signor, 46
Mayeure, Signor, 66
Mazziotti, Antonio, 6, 50, 56: breaks oath of silence, 21; contract guarantee, 80; contract with Leone, 78; departure for Lisbon, 25; disparaged by Giardini, 7; engaged by Leone as first man, 6; in King's Theatre roster for 1763-64, 12; maximum salary to be offered, 40; paid £84 by Rich, 25; party to lawsuit, vi, 21; petitions to testify in Italian, 26; salary, 27; salary advance, 20; to be auditioned, 40; voice disparaged by Walpole, 7
McVeigh, Simon, vii, 2-3, 17
Michel, Pierre Bernard, 11, 52: contract with Marcucci, 70

Middlesex, Lord, v, 1
Milan, 5, 38, 40, 44, 48, 56, 64, 66: Collegio dei Nobili Longone, 38; S. Sempliciano, 38; Teatro Ducale, 40
Mingotti, Regina, 1, 26: calls Baini a very indifferent singer, 9; calls Mazziotti a middling singer, 8; co-manager in 1756-57, 2; engaged by Giardini, 8; in King's Theatre roster for 1763-64, 12; not in management in 1763-64, 3; singing attacked by Walpole, 8; testimony on oath of silence, 21; to be hired by Giardini, 60
Modena, 52
Montefiascone, 40
Montpellier, 12
Mora: See Formigli
Morris and Caffarena, 62, 80
Morris, Giuseppe, 44, 46
Mozart, Leopold: reports Giardini's bankruptcy, 27; reports Manzuoli's salary, 27
Mozart, Wolfgang Amadeus: at Spring Garden in 1764, 48; *finta giardiniera, La*, 44; *Lucio Silla*, 57; *re pastore, Il*, 44
Munich, 44

Naples, 5-9, 11, 16, 19-20, 38, 40, 44, 48, 50, 54, 56, 58, 62, 64, 70, 78, 80, 82, 84: Teatro S. Carlo, 11, 40, 44-46
Nivernois, Duke of, 3
Noferi, Giovanni Battista, 48-50, 52, 54: in King's Theatre roster for 1763-64, 13

Offenbach, Jaques: *Les contes d'Hoffman*, 53
Orfeo: See Gluck
Orione: See Bach
Orsi and Company, 27
Orvietto, 48
Ottani, Gaetano, 10

Padua, 38, 48
Palladino, Giuseppe, 5, 38
Pamela: See Richardson
Paris, 3-5, 11, 13, 19, 25, 28, 44, 46, 50, 52, 54, 56, 68, 70, 72: Comédie Italienne, 48, 70
pasticcios, 1, 3, 5, 14, 40, 44, 56, 60: Vento's objections to composing, 15
pay-scale for opera personnel, 27
Pellegrini, Nicola, 9, 20
Pembroke, Lord, 76
Peretti, Niccolò: in King's Theatre roster for 1763-64, 12
Petrobelli, Pierluigi, 10, 44
Petty, Frederick C., 16
Piccinelli, Anna Maria, 52, 56
Piccinni, Niccolò, vi, 3-4, 14-15, 44, 56, 58, 60: *astrologa, L'*, 41; *Didone abbandonata*, 40; Leone to hire if possible, 14; music included in *Senocrita*, 15; music to be commissioned from, 14; popularity of *La buona figliuola*, 26; proposed salary, 27; terms offered by Giardini, 40; unavailable for 1763-64, 14
Pietro: See Sodi, Pietro
Piossasque, Joseph, Count: testimony on oath of silence, 21
Pozzi, Antonietta Cerocchi, 51-52
Prasca, Abbé, 44, 48
Price, Curtis, 14
Prussia, King of, 9-10, 50, 64
Public Advertiser: statement of 'requisites' for opera, 29

Quarantotto, Marquis, 64

Raaff, Anton, 10
Ravaschiello: See De Bustis, Vincenzo
re pastore, Il: See Mozart, W. A.
recruitment: questions about, v
Reggio Emilia, 46, 69
Rich, Sir Robert, vi, 17, 24: alleged author of *Réponse*, 24; attempt to take over King's Theatre, 25; ironic dedication of pamphlet to, 24; misidentifies Giardini's catch, 25
Richardson, Samuel: *Pamela*, 26
Riche de la Pouplinière, Le, 25, 72
Rinaldi, M., 37
Robinson, John William, vii
Rolfi, Francesco, 38: disrecommended, 46
Romani (tenor), 9-10, 19, 48, 50, 56, 58: unavailable, 64
Rome, 5, 8, 14, 16, 40, 44, 54, 56, 58, 62, 66: Teatro Alibert o delle Dame, 48-49, 52; Teatro Argentina, 39-41, 44, 48-49
Rosselli, John, 20, 41
Rule of Augmentation, 42

Sadie, Stanley, viii
salary scale for King's Theatre, 27
Salzburg, 44
Sartori, Angiola, 23, 26, 48, 56: goes to Lisbon for 1765-66, 25; hired by Giardini, 50; house in Paris, 72, 74; in King's Theatre roster for 1763-64, 12; leaves London for Paris, 50; recommends singers to Giardini, 48; salary unknown, 27; signed by Giardini as second woman, 5; witnesses Graziani's agreement, 74
Sartori, Claudio, viii
scene painter, 13, 64
Scolari, Giuseppe: *Statira*, 38
Senocrita (pasticcio), 15
Siena, 6, 44
Soderini, Mons, 76
Sodi, Pietro, 48, 52, 68: ballet master at King's Theatre for 1763-64, 13; demotes Marcucci, 12

93

Spagnioli, Clementina, 8, 44-45, 50, 56, 58, 60: letter to Leone, 60; to be offered up to 1400 zecchini, 46
Spiletta, La: See Giordani, Nicolina
Spilsbury, James: King's Theatre treasurer for 1763-64, 13
Stainton, Major, 76
Stone, George Winchester, Jr., viii

Tagnoni, Maddalena, 68-69: goes to Lisbon for 1765-66, 25; in King's Theatre roster for 1763-64, 12
Tartini, Giuseppe, 53
Taylor, William, v: on season for making engagements, 3
Ten Commandments, 4, 42
Tenducci, Giusto Ferdinando, 8: pleases subscribers in 1764-65, 28
Testone, Gio., 66
Tetley, Elizabeth: on King's Theatre roster for 1763-64, 13
Todi, Signor, 48, 50, 56
Tozzi: See Bianchi
travel expenses: payment forbidden, 6
Trombetta, Joseph, 2: announces retirement from management, 2; leaves England, 3, 48
Turin, 4, 19, 44, 46, 64: Teatro Regio, 10

Vanneschi, Francesco, 1-2
Varanellis, the (dancers), 44
Varese, Agostino Domenico, 44: letter to Leone, 62
Venice, 8, 11-12, 14-15, 44, 46, 52, 56, 71, 86: Teatro S. Angelo, 49; Teatro S. Benedetto, 44-45, 49, 69; Teatro S. Cassiano, 41, 46, 49; Teatro S. Giovanni Grisostomo, 49, 69; Teatro S. Moisè, 11, 39, 41, 46, 69; Teatro S. Salvatore, 46, 49; Teatro S. Samuele, 39, 45, 49
Venier, Jean Baptiste, 58
Vento, Mattia, vi, 14, 66: Burney's assessment of, 19; contractual duties, 15, 60; *Egiziana, L'*, 46; employed to cancel Baini's contract, 16; first contract with Leone, 16, 86; hired by Leone, 14; in King's Theatre roster for 1763-64, 12; *Leucippo*, 9, 15-16; objects to being called 'pasticiere', 15; paid in full for 1763-64, 17; paid £36 by Rich, 25; party to lawsuit, vi; petitions to testify in Italian, 26; plays harpsichord at opera performances, 16; retained as house composer in 1764, 28; salary, 27; salary advance, 20; salary and duties, 44; second contract with Leone, 16, 88; terms of employment, 56; to be hired in lieu of Piccinni, 14; unable to produce copy of contract, 16; view of pasticcios, 15; 1770 concert series with Giardini, 17
Vienna, 10-11, 52, 54, 56: Burgtheater, 40
Visconti, Radegonda, 5
Viterbo, 40
von Asow, E. H. Müller, 21

Walpole, Horace: criticizes Mazziotti's voice, 7; criticizes Mingotti's singing, 8; describes offer for Dauberval, 28; sour view of Giardini, 7
Weaver, Norma Wright, 41
Weaver, Robert Lamar, 41
Wiel, Taddeo, viii
Willaert, Saskia, 1
Wills and Leigh, 58, 64, 66, 82

Zampieri, Domenico ('il Domenichino'): picture by, 20
Zanaida: See Bach